Unna You Fullas

Unna You Fullas

GLENYSE WARD

First published by Magabala Books Aboriginal Corporation
Broome Western Australia 1991

Magabala Books receives financial assistance from the Government of Western Australia through the Department for the Arts; the Aboriginal and Torres Strait Islander Commission; and the Australia Council, the Federal Government's arts funding and advisory body.
Grateful acknowledgement is made for the support of Apple Computer Australia in the provision of Apple Macintosh equipment.

Copyright © Glenyse Ward 1991

All rights reserved. Apart from any fair dealing for the purposes of private study, research, criticism or review, as permitted under the Copyright Act, no part of this publication may be reproduced by any process whatsoever without the written permission of the author and the publisher.

Designer Carol Tang Wei
Editor Peter Bibby
Production Coordinator Merrilee Lands
Illustrations by Monica Lee
Printed by Australian Print Group, Maryborough, Victoria
Typeset in 11pt New Century

National Library of Australia
Cataloguing-in-Publication data

Ward, Glenyse, 1949–
Unna You Fullas.

ISBN 0 9588101 9 2.
1. Ward, Glenyse, 1949– –Fiction. I. Title.

A823.3

Thanks to the Aboriginal Arts Unit of the Australia Council for their generous assistance towards the development of *Unna You Fullas,* and to the management and staff of Magabala Books for their time and patience in making my second book possible.

G.W.

Grateful acknowledgement is made for permission to print words from songs: on p150, *Kookaburra Sits In The Old Gum Tree* by Marion Sinclair, by kind permission of the copyright owners, Larrikin Music Publishing Pty Ltd, Sydney; on p152, *The Happy Wanderer* by E. Moller, W. Moller and A. Ridge, by permission EMI Music Publishing Australia Pty Ltd, PO Box C156, Cremorne Junction, NSW 2090; on pp 173-75, *Jinny Come Lately* by Bryan Hyland, used by permission of Polygram Music Publishing Pty Ltd.

Also by Glenyse Ward

Wandering Girl

Contents

The Old Grey Ute	1
Settling In	3
Mud Pies	5
Banner	8
Winter Winds	11
Shoulders Apart	14
Singing	18
Make Me Pretty Kid	20
The Laundry Ghost	22
Lost	26
In the Kitchen	30
Changing of Duties	34
Watch Out for Sister	37
Albertus	42
The Only Father I Knew	45
My Secret	49
Now We Have to Go to Confession	56
Don't Cry You Fullas	64
The Runaways	72
Especially to zer Ringleaders	84
Can You See zer Bullet?	88
Brother Coming!	93
Real Solid and Neat	98
Koondang	106
A New One to Us	113
He Might Come in Here	116
What Is the Matter with You Lot?	124
Poppy	130

When the Fights Started	133
Prayers	137
I Didn't Feel Like Singing	143
The Concert	148
Read Your Story	153
Everyone Roared	157
Through the Door	160
How Long Were You Girls Here?	164
Changes	168
Jinny Come Lately	172
The Nativity	177
Glossary	182

For Nellie Buddah, my grandmother, taken from her
birthplace Liveringa; for Brian Ocean, my brother,
who was raised on another mission; for the father
I did not meet; and for my mother. For all
Aboriginal people who have lost their
families and are still searching.

The Old Grey Ute

The old grey ute kept chugging along the endless highway. Then we made our way down a winding bush track, a cloud of dust behind us. I had left St John of God's orphanage in the city. I was about five years old. The driver was Father Albertus, a German priest, and beside him sat Brother Roland, who bought me ice-cream and kept me amused with little games and antics. I sat between them. Brother was plump and cheery, with red rosy cheeks and a large belly protruding from his fat short frame.

This brother had an unusual object sticking out of his mouth. Every now and again I couldn't see his face for all this white substance, which had a strong smell. I just about choked. I thought it was fun and laughed and clapped my hands together until it cleared and I could see his big red face again.

The grey ute stopped outside a huge building and Br Roland sat me on his lap, turned me towards the window of the car and wound it down. I screamed and started sobbing uncontrollably, as all I could see was a mass of black grinning faces, and white teeth. Their arms were outstretched and their hands tugged at the sleeve of my dress. I clung tighter to Br Roland crying, "I want you, I want you!"

Two in the crowd pushed and shoved one another, trying to take me off Brother's lap. There was this fair head kid, a desert blonde, crying and grabbing my hand saying, "My sister, my sister!" She was seven years old and had been in St John of God's. About five others from the group, who were all older than me, had been there too and they cried out, remembering me.

Then Brother opened the car door in the midst of the bunch of girls and they swamped around us so much I just about suffocated with all their hugging. I was lifted up into someone's arms and quietened down a bit. All I could see was a smiling face, very close to mine, with blue cloth draped over her head. I came to know her as Sister Gertrude. She passed me over to a big girl from the group, who soaked my dress with tears and squeezed me nearly to death.

Then the big girl knelt down with me so that the smaller girl who had been pushing and shoving with the desert blonde, could give me a big slopping kiss on the cheek. Little did I know that the big girl who was crying and the little girl who kissed me were my natural sisters. They were Nita and Sally.

Right from the start that nun Sr Gertrude would give me to Nita, who was so much older than me she would mother me. Whenever I trotted off somewhere, she would come with me. She carried me round everywhere and if someone picked me up, she would come and grab me off them with, "Come to me, sister." You know how you hold out your hands to a baby? At night time she would come and tuck me in. When I was older she told me that she was my big sister. She had grown up at Moore River settlement.

Nita was considered a working girl at the age of fourteen. She left the mission to work for white people when I was seven. Sally, who was then eight years old, spent a lot longer with me, growing up with all the other girls round about the same age as us. We all considered one another sisters.

Settling In

I started to settle in with my new-found family. We grew up amongst many German influences in a very military-style fashion. Our dresses were all made out of khaki material, full-length, right down to the ankles, with long pockets and rick-rack around the hems. We did not have much choice in the colour of our woollen jumpers, they were either grey or brown. Our feet were usually bare. Only on Sundays we put on socks and sandals. In the later years we were given our first pair of school shoes.

As for the comfortable side of things, our sleeping place was a big dingy room, where old wooden double-decker beds stood side by side in two rows, which ran the length of the dormitory. Our mattresses were all made out of ticking material and filled with kapok. We never sank into a bed of feathers. They were so thin we could have just laid on the boards.

We grew accustomed to the sound of rattling keys in the morning, as Sister Ursula opened the lock on our dormitory door, and swung the cowbell in her vigorous striking hands. She was the Mother Superior. The sound was deafening. We automatically stumbled out of bed on the wooden floorboards, lowering our heads in reverence and reciting after Mother Superior our thankyou prayers to God for our comfortable night's sleep.

Something I've learnt to do is make beds by instinct. We'd have to make our beds up under the hawk eyes of Mother Superior, then stand back in a line and wait for her to inspect them. She would stalk around each bed looking for signs like sheets hanging over the edge or blankets loose, or if the pillow wasn't puffed up. Any bit of grey army blanket left hanging out over the side and Sister would pull the whole bed up and we'd suffer the consequences — miss out having breakfast.

After this we collected our bloomers from the bed-post.

These we scrubbed every night and hung there so Mother Superior could inspect them. They were made out of self-raising flourbags, Dingo brand. Our lockers were situated on the right-hand side of the dormitory. We'd identify our lockers by the numbers on them, 1 to 50. Mine was 23, the number given to me by the nuns.

From our lockers we collected our bundles of clothes, formed a line and followed Mother Superior, marching out of the dormitory, through this room we'd called the Little Dining Room. On the right was another room partitioned off as a dispensary. We'd pass through the kitchen, then turn to our left and Mother Superior would throw open a flywire door to lead us outside. There was this bit of a hill we had to march down to a corrugated iron shack, which served as a bathroom. There were basins on one side of the wall, toilets on the other. In the middle stood two long benches, where we sat and waited with our bundles. A great tin wash tub stood in the corner. The nuns used to warm the water in kettles on the kitchen stove and carry them down to the bathroom shed to blend with cold water in the tub.

Later, when I was eleven, two big combustion stoves were put at the back of the shed, with large water tanks built over them. The working girls had the job of keeping these boilers filled with wood. From then on we had showers. We stood in line with our towels, the little ones waiting for a turn in the tub, the big ones waiting for a turn at the four showers. Two girls could shower together behind a plastic curtain. They didn't have long, and tried to grab as much hot water as they could, especially on cold mornings.

From age six to eleven, I was given baths by Sister in the old tub, with a big cake of sandsoap and a stiff scrubbing brush. Amidst our cries of pain she'd go to work on our elbows and knees.

Mud Pies

I'd been at my new home two years when I turned seven in 1956. I was well and truly used to the girls with whom I would grow up. Poppy was the blonde kid who came running up to me on the very first day I arrived, holding her hands out and calling, "My sister." She was a bit of a sookie and stuttered a lot, which made me angry. I used to get so frustrated listening to her.

At night in the dormitory laying back on our wooden double-decker beds, us other girls would be trying to get some sleep but all you could hear coming from Poppy's bed was creak, creak. She had a bad habit of rocking her head from side to side before she fell asleep. Because our beds were old and wooden, as soon as you touched them they would wobble and creak. I remember how the older girls would get up and give her a flogging, to shut her up, which only made matters worse. She would start crying. We'd put our kapok pillows over our heads to drown out the prolonged, inarticulate, confused cry of pain.

Then there were Meryl, Thelma and Florry who were all natural sisters. Meryl was older than her other two sisters. She was a working girl like my sister Nita; I really liked her as she used to pet me up. She used to give her sisters special things like an extra sandwich or a piece of apple she would sneak out of the kitchen while helping Sr Gertrude. I'd get the same. When I'd miss out, I'd automatically go and fight her younger sister Florry for whatever she had. There was something about Florry I could not stand. Every time we looked at one another we'd clash.

Thelma and Florry were lean, long-legged, scrawny girls. They both had problems with their eyes, so they were forever squinting and bumping into things and couldn't read what was written on the blackboard. The nuns organised a couple of doctors to come from Perth to look at our eyes. They lifted our eyelids and asked if our eyes were hurting. They examined our pupils and held up cards for us to read. Thelma and Florry had a lot of trouble with the cards and they were both provided with glasses shortly after that.

Sometimes us girls would play at the back of the old tin shack which was our bathroom, making mud pies. For our moulds we used empty oblong sardine tins and half-round salmon tins, which we found in the dump and filled with mud. Then with a quick movement of the wrist we'd turn the tin upside down, and our pies would be standing upright on a flat piece of board, which we used to have laying right beside us on the ground. Sometimes we'd get Florry to hold onto our mud pies while we arranged our board to make more room to squeeze more mud pies on.

Florry had this terrible habit. When she wanted to go to the toilet she'd hang on till the last minute and wet herself. When she couldn't hold on any more, she'd cross her legs and start jumping up and down, whimpering and crying, and her glasses would fog up. Then she'd have to drop whatever she had in her hands, to clean her glasses, because she could hardly see without them. Therefore she'd muck up our mud pies by dropping them and dancing up and down on our board, saying she couldn't see! I think we made her habit worse with the floggings we gave her. Years later she became my best friend.

One of my great joys of growing up in the mission was going for picnics in Our Lady's Truck. It was an old Bedford with cattle-sides on the open tray, that had been blessed as Our Lady's, in honour of the Virgin Mary. I remember when we first got the truck, we had a special day for the christening of it. The nuns and brothers said that Our Lady would protect us on our picnics and excursions into the city.

Our Lady's Truck was driven by Br Edward, who would put a ladder up for us kids to climb aboard. We squatted down and one of the nuns used to sit with us on a chair which was secured to the bars. Off we'd go to Pumphrey's Bridge or into Perth to look at the firestation. We were driven around everywhere in Our Lady's Truck. On our trips to Perth we would stand up, hanging onto the sides and the rails, singing and shouting in delight at all the tall buildings and different kinds of cars, waving at passers-by on the roadside. We used to get a lot of stares whenever Brother stopped in the traffic or at intersections. We never took notice, we were so happy and excited getting away from the mission.

Nita came to say goodbye to me one morning before school.

"Don't worry, little sis, one day we'll all meet up again, when we leave here. Don't worry, you've still got Banner and Sally and all the other mob."

It never dawned on me during the day that my eldest sister was going for good. At night, lying in my bed, I cried myself to sleep. As weeks turned into months, I got used to not seeing Nita, but I missed her.

Banner

Banner was removed from her parents like us and she was put into the same orphanage, St John of Gods. Her mother was of Aboriginal descent and her father was a black American. At ten, Banner was the oldest of our group. Built like a man, she had a commanding influence over us. Her behaviour was overbearing sometimes. Us little girls used to sit back like timid mice. She was boisterous and rough in her manners and never had a care in the world.

Even though she was the instigator when there was trouble, she was very good at bribing. Somewhere along the line, we ended up taking her punishment. I remember Banner used to have tight curly black hair. Even to this day, I still cannot think what Banner's reason was for rubbing soap in her hair and leaving it there. Every time we'd have a bath or wash, Banner used to break a piece of Relax soap and rub it into her hair until it was real soapy. Then she'd get a comb and comb it all back.

When we used to go down to the dam for a swim, we'd play this game, Brandy in the water. About four of us would duck down, hold our breath and crawl along the muddy floor of the dam. When we were running out of air, we'd pop up on the other side or wherever, depending on how good we were at holding our breath. The remaining girl would be waiting to hit us with a tennis ball. Once you were hit, then it would be vice versa.

Banner was always the first to get caught. Some places the water was murky and some places clear, but all the girl with the ball had to do was trace Banner's head, because the soap used to run out leaving a trail of white foamy bubbles. So that made us laugh about Banner.

The other two girls who were in our group were Lynn and Lola Neal. Their brother Jimmy was the first boy to arrive in the mission, a couple of years later. Lola was in the older age group. Us girls never liked her, because she used to think she was a nun. She followed the nuns around and copied how they talked to us. Lola was put in charge of us by Sr Ursula, if we were out in the fields playing a game of rounders or skittles, whatever the game would be. She'd be standing on the sideline watching like a hawk at everything we'd say and do. Lola would hardly ever join in.

Sometimes we'd make a slip and drop the ball and say, "Bum," or copy some of the older girls' words, what we'd hear them say, "Bloody" or "Jesus Christ." Soon as Lola would hear that she'd carry on like Sr Ursula, start clapping her hands from the sideline, shouting like mad, with her hands raised in the air.

"Stop the game! Girls, I heard what somebody said. Now who was it?" And she immediately started calling our names out, "Was it you, Sprattie, or Banner, or Sally?"

"I never said anything, Lola, ask Banner, she might of heard someone." Us girls acted dumb and made out that we weren't aware as to what was going on, as usual. We carried on blaming one another, and a big fight started.

Banner said to Florry, "Did you say something?" Then Florry looked at my sister.

"I never heard nothing, unna, Sally?"

"Gurn, don't you look at me and blame me, I'll slap your face," Sally retorted and because it was common in the mission days to take it up for your sister when there was trouble, Florry's other sister, Thelma, told my sister, "You leave my sister alone. If you hit her, I'll punch you and knock you flying."

"I'd like to see you try it!" One thing about Sally, she wouldn't back down from anyone. Especially if the challenge was put to her. "Come on Thelma, you make the first hit, but don't miss me, because see those glasses you got on, Thelma, I'll break them in bits, and make you and your bony-legged sister Florry jump and piss."

Then Lola butted in, and put our game to an end, because we'd all committed a sin. No-one would own up to Lola and because of our fighting and arguing, we were marched off to Sr Ursula. Mainly we would find her in the dormitory, mending our clothes, or checking that our lockers were in order.

Having done her duty by delivering us to Sr Ursula, and giving a rundown on our sins committed in the fields, Lola left us in Sr Ursula's hands. Sister gave us a lecture for what seemed hours. I felt really sick in my stomach after one of Sr Ursula's lectures. They left me with a feeling of being no good. We were sent off to the kitchen and made to peel buckets and buckets of potatoes for our punishment.

Winter Winds

The winter winds were howling, rattling at the old wooden window panes. Rushes of cold air entered through the gaps in the building. A gloomy shadow hung over the vast, eerie dormitory. I used to hate waking up on these cold frosty winter mornings. I hated the winter months. They used to dampen my spirits.

This particular morning made no exception, my whole body felt like a bad case of rigor mortis had set in; the grey army blanket must have slipped off during the night. I regained possession of it and painstakingly worked into a crouching position in the middle of my wobbly wooden double-decker bed.

Quite often I would be relieved waking up in that unstable bed, knowing that it was still standing and I was lying in it. I glanced around the dormitory at all the other girls sleeping peacefully. I could put up with aches, knowing that the daylight had come, as the spooky shadows disappeared into the night. I looked down the long corridor of the dormitory, to where the kerosene lamp was standing in the vastness of the brick fireplace. The flame was almost burned down.

It wasn't too scary, as I could see all the objects around me quite clearly, which otherwise would have been quite frightening to my young mind. The darkness terrified me, because the older girls told the little girls ghostie yarns. We used to be paralysed with terror at night-time.

An older girl would pull one of the curtains aside to show us the lights up in the hills, saying they were redeyes making their camps. If you could see the redeyes, they could see you, they were the mumaries looking at you, like red coals burning.

We'd gasp, "Waa ...!" and the big girl would quickly let the curtain fall, telling us that if we were naughty, the little hairy men would come with their big sacks, pick us up and take us away so we would never be seen again. The little men were the mumaries that lived in big caves. We could see caves in the hills in the daytime. The little girls went back to their beds sobbing their hearts out, too frightened to cry out loud, for fear the mumaries might come and get them.

The nuns told us that if we were frightened of the dark or the devil we didn't believe in God, and in times of trouble, or if we needed help we'd have to pray to God. "He will help you." So with a confused mind I'd stop my crying and pray.

"Please God don't let the mumaries come out and get us. I never did anything wrong, I never swore today, I did all my jobs, and tomorrow I'll be even better." Sometimes I used to think God was a devil too because he never answered me, and I couldn't see him.

Cold shivers ran down my spine as I caught a breath of freezing wind. My pyjama top wasn't close fitting. With trembling hands and teeth chattering I raised myself up to a kneeling position to secure the top around my body. I got rid of some old tin buttons which were hanging loosely off it and tied a few knots down the middle.

Lying flat on my back I lifted my bottom, pulled my baggy pyjama pants up over my waist and tied the string twice in a knot. I gathered up the blanket, wrapped it firmly around my shivering body, curled up and went back to sleep. All too soon our morning slumber was disturbed by the rattling of keys.

"Time to get up!"

Some of the girls were slow to get out. Some had woken up in a wet bed. Apart from being embarrassed and shamed, they were shown no mercy and no exception was made. With clammy pyjamas clinging to their bodies they knelt down too.

The smell was sickening. I glanced across and saw Mother Superior stripping one bed. Everything came off. With one hand she held her nose in two fingers. With the other she wrenched the wet sheets from the bed.

"Ach, you vill get up and take sheets to laundrin," she told the shivering girl. "Kommit madchen, los los aufstehn!"

There was a lot of sniggering. We couldn't help but laugh at Mother Superior's comical speech, although we felt sorry for our mates. After prayers we scurried around making our beds and getting everything in order. I gave my pillow a few punches to get it all even, like kneading dough for bread as the kapok used to sink in.

When our beds were made we lined up along one side of the dormitory in front of the lockers. I was waiting and hoping that I had done everything right. By this time we all had one thought going through our minds, and that was food. I dreaded the thought of missing out. A couple of girls' beds were stripped that morning — I could imagine how they felt. With a silent prayer I thanked God for letting me have breakfast.

Shoulders Apart

The frost around us looked like the pictures of snow in my reading book. We were all clean and Mother Superior had marched us from the bathroom and formed us into rows of ten for our morning exercises. We soon started shivering again. Mother Superior would insist that back in Germany, where she came from, they always did exercise on freezing, snowy mornings to get their blood circulating.

While we stood "shoulders apart", Mother Superior would check each line to see if all the girls were standing upright, chest out and hands down beside their bodies, clenched in a fist. Then we'd wait for her to march down to the front and stand before us girls.

"Komm! Madchen! Ein, zwein, drier, vier, funf, sechs, sieben, acht, neun, zelm!" She roared at the top of her voice and we followed her actions, as she threw her fists up in the air, then down beside her body, counting to ten.

"Ein, zwein, drier ..." we recited along with her bellowing, following her pattern of movements. After a vigorous workout, we'd march up the hill and over to the dining room, a hundred yards away. There we stood in a straight line in front of the dining room stairs and Mother Superior went away to the convent to have her breakfast, leaving us there in the charge of another nun just as strict.

Under the watchful eye of Sr Ursula we'd clamber up the stairs and enter the dining room. We tried not to be hasty, walking automatically around the long benches to our places. There we stood facing one another across the tables for the blessing. Sister started us off, "Oh Lord for what we are about to receive ..."

Then we all sat down and waited impatiently for our turn to go to the serving table, where Sister and one of the bigger working girls handed out our plastic bowl of semolina and a piece of buttered bread. Back at our tables, we'd eat this slowly, so it would last longer. A working girl made up the tea in a huge pot with the milk and sugar already in it, and poured this into enamel pitchers, setting out two to each table.

Sr Ursula walked around our tables. When she saw everyone was finished she ordered us to stand and recite after her our thankyous to God.

"Bless us Oh Lord for these and all the other gifts which of Thy Bounty we have received, through Christ Our Lord Amen."

Outside the dining room, we all scattered to do our duties like robots. Every girl from the smallest to the biggest had a job to do. There were ten girls in the kitchen, under the supervision of Sr Gertrude the cook. She was a fiery person and all work had to be done in silence when Gertrude was around.

Two girls were allocated to washing all the pots. In another section three girls cleaned all the bowls and cups. Along the bench two seven-year-olds washed the cutlery. Over on the other side of the kitchen three girls washed and wiped the Fathers' dishes separately, because their meals were served on china plates, cups and saucers. Their eating quarters were attached to ours and to get to them you had to walk down a small passage. On the right was their Little Dining Room and on the left facing it the Visitors' Room, which served farmers and their families, when they came to church on Sunday.

Both of these rooms had shutter-like antique doors which opened out on a rounded balcony overlooking the playing fields. The balconies were made out of quarry rock and on each side was a flight of steps. This was the way the brothers and priests came in and out, back-way to their monastery, instead of going through our dining room.

The three girls cleared away the dishes from the fathers' table and took them down to the kitchen for washing up. All the tables had to be scrubbed and the blue willow-pattern plastic tablecloths wiped and put back dry. Then the wooden floors were waxed and polished until they shone.

Two girls cleaned the dormitories, waxing the old floorboards, and two more the toilets. Later, when there were more girls, the number on each job increased. At that time there were no washing machines in the laundry, so there had to be lots of laundry girls.

The eldest used to light up the coppers outside and boil the clothes, using the stirring sticks to get the clothes out, hooking them into oval tin tubs with handles. These were dragged into the laundry, where ten troughs were fixed to the wall, going halfway round the room. Other girls would stand washing boards in the troughs to scrub the clothes after the boiling. Then we'd hang out the washing on long lines, with props to keep them up.

For a while I worked in the dairy, helping the brothers, along with ten other girls. Brother Edward was a boisterous sort of person, very tall, with glasses and baggy pants, held up with braces. He had big army boots and socks and always wore a hat. He was like Mother Superior and never missed a trick. Br Roland made us laugh every time we looked at him. He was chubby, with a big pot belly, pants like Br Edward, at half mast, hobnailed boots and wide-brimmed hat. He also smoked a pipe and his nature was quite cheerful compared to the rest of them.

Brother Victor was tall, with a ring of hair around his scalp but bald in the middle. There was something about him that made him different from the rest. He was never aggressive and when in his company I wasn't nervous or frightened. I felt at peace. He had the most gentle blue eyes and I used to think that he was Saint Vincent Pallotti. We had a big painting of St Vincent on our dormitory wall and Br Victor was the dead image of it, forever smiling, never a harsh word for us kids. When we saw him we would hang on his hands. It might be around the dairy, or feeding pigs and chickens.

I remember how, when we saw him, us girls would run like mad, shouting, "Brother, I'll carry the bucket for you." And for a moment he wouldn't utter a word, just smile and put down his bucket, or whatever he was carrying. Then he would hold his hands out.

"Komm children."

We must have given him the willies, because we'd all go off squabbling and fighting as to who got Brother first, and who should be carrying the bucket.

Singing

Every last Saturday of the month at the mission, we used to have singing practice with Sister Erika, who was very tall and attractive with blue serene eyes. From the few locks that escaped at the front of her veil I could see that her hair was a soft light yellow. I thought she spoiled her looks when she became upset with us for making mistakes. The songs that we had to learn were mainly for the church services the following day and all through the month.

Sr Erika used to take her singing to heart, not one mistake to be made, otherwise we would have to go over the same verse until it was perfect. This was in Latin. All our hymns were sung in Latin, not that it mattered to me, for my heart was never in singing practice. I found it so boring and frustrating to be shouted at by Sister and pulled and shoved, getting my cheek pinched for making mistakes. I used to love playing by myself on the piano which stood in the far corner of our dining room, where all the practices were held. But after some of our wild sessions with Sister, that turned me right off playing music.

It was a wonder the piano wasn't smashed to bits by Sister's hard pounding, her fingers beating down on the keys. Sometimes during our lessons I used to wonder, why does she have to get so upset all the time? We were told every day that God loves everyone, sinners and all. As far as I was concerned, He still loved us for all our mistakes. So why should Sister get so upset?

The time I liked hearing Sister sing was on our walks in the bush. I used to love going up into the hills and sitting on a big rock, to gaze into the distance at the sweeping plains ahead. Everything was so green and peaceful.

We girls would squat down on rocks with our dresses pulled over our knees, making a bit of a hollow in the middle, where our berries would lie in a bunch. While we'd eat the berries from our laps, Sister would stand on a rock and cup her hands around her mouth and yodel. The mission was a hilly place, with gullies and valleys everywhere. Her yodelling used to echo back to us in a thousand voices, making us laugh and feel happy.

Looking back on it now, after having taught my own two kids the folk songs we used to sing, and having listened to them singing songs like that, I understand how she must have felt, going through the routine of teaching us *Kookaburra Sits in the Old Gumtree* and *The Happy Wanderer*.

Sr Erika would tell us of her homeland, the Swiss Alps, and of snow. I understand how she must have felt when she stood on the rocks at the mission and yodelled for us. There must have been a real longing for her home, and it would have seemed strange to her, having tall redgum trees, blue skies, singing birds and dark-skinned, snotty-nosed kids jumping up laughing and shouting for joy around her.

Make Me Pretty Kid

One of our jobs was to work out in the paddock, dragging a sack and picking up cow dung for the nuns' gardens around the convent. Ever since I was little I had often marvelled at the old building. It was made out of quarry rocks and built by Italians. It looked like a castle. The convent was out of bounds to us kids. The only time we were allowed inside was to attend church, because there was a chapel in the grounds.

When we collected cow dung for the gardens we'd be at it most of the day. The nuns would ring the bell and we'd go in for dinner, then start off again. I hated picking up dung. Poppy, Thelma and I worked together, taking it in turns, chucking the dry pieces into the bag, and shovelling the fresh ones up into the old wheelbarrow. Then one of us would wheel the barrow a mile up to the convent, unload it and go for another lot. Some of the bigger girls were there to help pack it in.

When it was my turn to take the load and dump it off, I wearily wheeled it back and flopped down on the ground beside the barrow. Meryl came over to me.

"Get up."

"I'm tired. I wish I was a working girl like you."

The working girls got away with a lot. All they seemed to do was supervise and boss us little ones around. She helped me lift the sack and walked beside the wheelbarrow as I returned to the paddock. When we were out of hearing distance from the nuns, Meryl spoke.

"Sprattie, you want to become a big girl and grow up fast, and have long hair? See that dung you are picking up? Look down there where those cows are, every time they go toilet, run down there and dive in it, and rub it all over you. Your hair will begin to grow long and you'll become big like me."

So while out scouting for my next load of dung with Poppy

and Thelma, I told them, "When you see a cow go, tell me." Poppy and Thelma were curious to know why. I told them.

"Meryl said I'll get long hair and I'll be a working girl."

Every now and then I'd get a yell from the two of them and they'd race over with me to a fresh patch of dung. They wanted to rub some on themselves too, because we all wanted to become big working girls.

"You're not allowed to," I said, "only me, because I asked first and because you two are lazy and you still got a lot of work to do."

By this time I was plastered in goona. All you could see was the whites of my eyes. I left Thelma and Poppy squashing flies from their faces as I stumbled and staggered with my big load up to the garden where Sister Birgit was standing.

She was a strange sort of person, who would smile when she was about to hit us. I found out when I grew older that she had a nervous complaint and the expression on her face came from what was boiling up inside. Her face used to change. We thought she was smiling when instead it was the other way round, she was fuming. When I reached the gate with my load I saw Sr Birgit smiling at me and I got happy inside too. Then she yelled at me.

"Ach, girl, leave zer vheelbarrow zhere and komm mit me over to laundrin!" She picked up a stick and held her nose up in the air. "Hurry up, girl!"

I started shaking cruel. Sr Birgit was very tall, with a heavy build, brown eyes and the strands of her brown hair would come out from underneath her veil when she was agitated. Every now and then I'd get a poke in the back from the stick. When we reached the laundry she couldn't wait to fill the old tub up, pulling faces at me.

"Take all your clothes off oontz jump in zer tob." I went through an agonising half hour while Sister took her frustration out on me with a cake of sandsoap and a scrubbing brush.

The Laundry Ghost

The laundry was apart from the main buildings and seemed half a mile away. It stood out alone surrounded by fenced-off paddocks where big woolly rams grazed. The little girls hated working there. It was dismal and eerie, with grey brick walls, red tiled roof and a wooden window on each side.

The big girls used to tell us that when they passed the laundry at night with the nuns, to go and pray in the shrine up in the hills, they saw the figure of a stooped old lady draped in white cloth, at one of the windows.

We were punished quite a lot in the mission for misbehaving. I could put up with the pain from a good hiding, because after a while the hurt faded away, but the punishment that stayed with me was the fear of being locked up in the laundry at night.

I remember one night Zelda, Banner and I were talking after lights out. Lola didn't like it, so being a bigger girl, she went down to the convent and came back with Sr Ursula, who was fuming mad.

"Girls, girls who vas talking? Get op!" Ursie's harsh voice hollered down the passage. Her hands twitched and rattled the bundle of keys as she stalked down the aisles between the rows of beds, like a lion hunting her prey. Of course as usual we were sound asleep like perfect little angels. Suddenly I felt Sister's finger and thumb grab my cheek and pinch it tight.

"Get op, Glenysen Sprattsen, I know you are avake, oontz zhat you vere talking!" I rose out of bed, rubbing my burning cheeks, as Sr Ursula stormed over to give Zelda and Banner the same treatment.

"Stand in zer aisle, girls." Sister pulled us by the ears and we went for a swing on her arm, squealing as she walked us around into line.

"Seeing you vant to talk all night oontz opset zer ozzers, you vill come mit me to zer laundrin where you vill darn socks, yah?" She took the lantern from the fireplace. "Komm follow me!"

Miserable, we followed behind her to the laundry, shivering in our thin pyjamas. The wind was blowing strong on the way over and twice the flame in the old lamp nearly went out.

At the laundry door Sr Ursula put the lamp down, unlocked the padlock and pushed the creaky door open. We stood huddled up together.

"Komm girls." She picked the lamp up. We followed her to a wide cane basket, with the sisters' and brothers' mending in it, standing in the middle of a big wooden table. We were all frightened. Sr Ursula shoved a light globe in each girl's trembling hands. "Get a move on, hurry up, you know vhere zer darning needles are kept, oontz zer black wool. Komm, komm," she clapped her hands and we went to a box for our darning needles. We pushed the light globe into a sock underneath the actual hole.

When Sr Ursula saw us propped up on the edge of the table ready to start darning, she went over to the far wall of the laundry and took an extra lamp down from a hook, lit it up, then turned around and glared at us.

"You girls vill sit here till two o'clock in zer morning oontz I vant most of zer socks done. If zhey are not darned properly you vill komm back tomorrow night oontz zer next oontz so on until zhey are done properly. Iss zhis understanding girls?"

"Yes, Sister."

It was about half-past nine when she left us. We heard the padlock and her footsteps on the gravel fading away, and we looked at one another in the light of the lantern. Then we had a hate session against Sr Ursula, something which was common amongst us. Growing up with the nuns we'd talk about them, and then find ourselves on our knees asking God for forgiveness, because we were taught that they were married to God in a spiritual way and if we said anything bad about them God would punish us.

The window panes were rattling and we could feel a cold draught. We bunched together around the lantern, so the wind wouldn't blow it out. There was a gap between the top of the walls and the old tile roof with its bare rafters. We became silent, until I blurted out, "Banner!" My voice started to shake. "Is it true about that ghostie lady, them big girls was telling us about?"

Banner glanced around the laundry. Zelda spoke in a hoarse whisper, "Keep quiet Sprattie, trust you to be thinking about what we're thinking too, unna Banner?"

"Yeah, don't make a sound you fullas, otherwise if that woman hear us, we're finished."

"Choo, don't talk like that Banner."

"Well keep quiet then."

I tried to concentrate on pressing the needle in hard over the rough parts of the sock.

We were all engrossed with our darning, when an eerie strange sensation filled the room. I felt my body go all weak and clammy. The wind strengthened and the howling seemed like someone crying. Quite suddenly this form appeared in front of us, draped in white, then disappeared again.

We came to our senses with Sr Ursula yelling from the open door of the laundry. "Girls, girls stop your screaming." She hurried over to us. "Vhat iss going on? Get op, stop your crying!"

"Sister we saw you, just like you were standing in front of us," Banner blurted out.

"Ach, girl don't be stupid."

She walked over to check our darning, and we noticed how pale her face went. "Ach girls," she said in a quiet voice, "you can do good vork vhen you put your mind to it." In a puzzled state, we followed Sister back to the dormitory. The next day we had to go back to the laundry for the inspection of our night's darning, with a nun standing by.

This time it was Sister Giselle who held up the socks and said that we had done a wonderful job. They were perfectly darned. We were shocked because we knew that we didn't darn at all, we just did one straight stitch through the hole and tried to hurry up the job and get out of there. We knew that this wasn't our work. I knew it especially when I didn't see the white cotton I had used.

Lost

We were accustomed to walks in the bush and one day it was Sr Giselle who came with us. She was still very new to the mission, just out from Germany.

It began a very hot and humid day but we loved our bush walks. Come rain or come shine, nothing could stop us. The place we were going to was a beautiful spot we had found ourselves. We called it The Springs. Big redgum trees stood tall there beneath a blue serene sky. The moss on the rocks was like a mound of green carpet all around.

Having reached our own springs we ran to the water and gulped it down. We sat gazing at the crystal water gushing over the rocks and the rainbow colours in the droplets on the leaves and branches. It must have rained not long before. Now it was so bright and peaceful, the singing and chirping of the birds mingling as they went along in their own world. I could feel in my body that spring was my favourite season, everything so fresh.

I looked at Sr Giselle as she sat down exhausted on a rock. Thinking she must be thirsty I bent down in front of her and cupped my hands, gesturing to Sister to drink. She was muttering something in German and pointing around with a worried look.

"Madchen, madchen — girls, girls."

I pointed to the bushes and tried to tell her that the girls had gone looking for berries. Then I left her and went off to collect some for myself. The bush there was prickly and we used a stick to beat through it and under it to reach the milk berries. I plucked some, showed Sr Giselle and ate one in front of her.

At first she was alarmed and said that I would die from poisoning but as I urged her to try one, she began to calm down and became convinced that everything was all right. She even consented to have a drink. Not long after that, Poppy and Florry came out of the thicket and sat down on the mossy rocks beside us. We started eating the berries they had collected. I called over to Poppy.

"Have you seen the rest of the girls?"

"Nah, only me and Florry was together."

Delia, a new girl to our group, Thelma, Banner, Marianne, Sally and Nettie, she had not seen. To us girls it was no worry if we never saw the other girls — we knew that we would catch up with them back at the mission. They'd probably gone ahead, although usually, on these walks with the nuns, everybody would meet back at the same spot from which we'd spread out for our rambles. Then we'd all walk back to the mission together through the bush.

It was getting late and became overcast. A big rain cloud covered the sun and made the atmosphere miserable. Giselle sang in her loudest voice, "Kommit heim!! Kommit heim!!"

At the end of our excursions, when we were ready to go, us girls often copied our German sisters and sang out, "Home time, home time, kommit heim!!" to any latecomers. If they heard us they would sing back, "We komming, we kommit heim!!" The sisters made us laugh.

Giselle sounded so funny calling the girls in her accent, that we bellowed over the top of her, in spite, to drown her voice. We didn't get into trouble because she thought we were helping her. If only she knew.

Still no sign of the girls. The raindrops were falling quite frequently now.

"Komm, komm, girls, ve vill go back to zer mission."

With anxious looks on our faces, we gathered round Sister.

We never spoke any more of the girls, as we rushed home to avoid getting soaked. Back at the mission we went about our normal duties, and had a hot bath before tea-time. Sr Giselle left us in the charge of a big girl and went to join the other nuns in the convent. I thought something was wrong, when only three of us smaller girls and the working girls sat down around the long table. All my other mates' places were empty.

When we were ready for bed, Sr Giselle took prayers and asked us to pray to God for the rest of the girls who were lost out in the bush, so they could come home safely. Then it hit us, they were lost. Poppy, Florry and myself started crying, because our mates and my sister Sally were three of the lost ones. Sister told us to be quiet and pray.

"You have to be strong girls, believe in God, with God all things are possible."

The rain was falling hard on the tin roof now, as us three and the older working girls all sat on a bed, clutching one another. A big girl held a lantern near us for comfort. Two of the older nuns, Sr Ursula and Sr Gertrude, went searching with two brothers and Fr Albertus in the direction of the springs. One of the nuns kept ringing the hand bell, hoping the girls might hear. In the meantime two of the nuns kept taking it in turns to ring the big bell called the Angelus.

When we'd go for our walks in the bush, and we'd hear the Angelus bell we'd have to kneel where we were and say prayers. No matter how far away from the mission, you could hear the bell. So all through the night we comforted one another as the nuns rang the bell, hoping to reach the girls.

It took us nearly all night to get to sleep. Every couple of hours a nun would check up on us. Then she'd say prayers with the bigger girls. I was drained out. I fell asleep amidst the prayers and ringing of the Angelus bell.

Next morning I woke to excited and shouting voices and kids tugging at my grey blanket and just about dragging me out of bed. I jumped up frightened because I was still half awake and half asleep. I realised it was Banner, Thelma and Sally. They were sopping wet. Sr Giselle was trying to get the girls away to dry them, while Poppy, Florry and I hugged them and cried. They had come home at last.

In the Kitchen

I used to like working in the kitchen, because there was plenty to do. I hated scrubbing the pots and pans but when it came to baking cakes, I'd be there. The nuns we worked under all seemed to have similar temperaments, hard as nails.

Sr Gertrude was fat and short. Different times I used to see strands of her golden blonde hair sticking out from under the veil. She had beautiful blue eyes and when she used to get angry her whole appearance changed. I thought of the witches in my Grimm's fairytale books. Hard as she was, I took a liking to her, although thinking back now, I was a real devil to her, and I couldn't understand why she got to like me in the end. I was a real brat and gave her hell.

It didn't matter to me if any of the other nuns hit me, then I'd have a good bawl, go and find one of my mates to play with, and think nothing of it. But when I was flogged by Sr Gertrude, I felt hurt deep down inside and I could not talk to her straight away. I used to sulk for days. It may have been because she was the nun I remembered from when I first arrived in the mission at five years old, the one who held and soothed me and wiped my tears away. She fed me a bowl of jelly and I never forgot that.

So I grew up with a sense of closeness, working beside Sr Gertrude. I used to think she was real great when every now and again she would give me a biscuit or something. In the kitchen amongst the other girls I thought I was a big shot when some of them called me Sister's pet, and I must admit that I played on it too. I used to set them up.

This one incident, Kelly was giving me hell. She was a bigger girl and bossed me around the kitchen, getting me to scrub her pots and pans. I never said anything, just kept scrubbing and wiping the sweat off my face.

Banner and Zelda were down the far end making bread and

dripping sandwiches. We used to love our bread and dripping!

This particular day Sr Birgit was working with Gertrude in the kitchen. Sr Birgit had that strange kind of temperament. When her emotions were stirred, she went quiet, and smiled. If we were going to cop it, she'd go very quiet, and grin. We knew the signs, when to put our hands over our heads, or cower down for protection.

Most of us had found out about Sr Birgit's strange moods the hard way. Now we were always aware of her presence around us and used to tread cautiously. But this was the first time Kelly was in the kitchen with her.

She kept shoving more pots than I could handle into the deep steel sink. My back was killing me. Being so small I had to stand on a stepping block and bend over. I straightened up for a breather and glanced around the kitchen. I could see Sr Birgit standing with her back to us, pouring out the mixture of a chocolate cake into a tray to bake it for the fathers' and brothers' morning tea. The nearest girl to me, Tessie, was peeling a bucket of potatoes.

We used sign language, so we wouldn't make it obvious. We weren't allowed to make noise or talk while we worked. "Choo," I whispered, "Tessie." She lifted her head up in the air a couple of times in a beckoning way, while she still worked her potato peeler with the wooden handle and jagged steel blade. I could read her lips saying, "What's up?" I clung to the edge of the sink with one hand, leaned out on my block and with my other hand pointed at Sr Birgit. I straightened up, shrugged my shoulders with both hands stretched out and rolled my eyes back towards Sister, which spelt out silently to Tessie.

"Where is Sister Gertrude?"

She caught on, and with her head up and lips pouted, she turned her head to the window just above her sink, meaning that Sister had gone down to the convent, which could be seen from Tessie's window. So I grabbed the cutting board. I wanted it for an excuse if Sr Birgit happened to look up and saw me going over to Banner.

"Where the hell do you think you're going?" Kelly snarled. It choked me up to answer her calmly, because by this time I was boiling, I'd had enough of her bullying me all morning. In my sweetest voice I said, "Kelly, I am taking this board over to Banner, I shan't be long." I felt her eyes go right through my back as I walked away.

Banner was up to her tricks again, having a good feed of bread and dripping, unseen by Sister. I thought she was really brave. "Here, Sprattie, have a piece."

"No, Banner, choo, Birgit will catch me, then I'll be finished." I took a big bite all the same and threw the rest back to her real quick-way. Then I told Banner how Kelly was treating me badly. Zelda overheard and moved closer.

"Sprattie, why don't you punch her in the mouth and shut her up? Just wait till I'm finished here, I'll take it up for you, I'll go over and knock her out for you. I don't care about Sister, no-one's going to touch my cobber." I stood there with my chest stuck out, feeling solid, when I heard Zelda say she would take up for me.

Banner got really wild.

"Get on with your own job," she told Zelda in a loud whisper, and then turned to me. "No-one's going to take it up for you, not even me. What have I been telling you all the years we've been growing up together? You are a big girl now, you get right back over there. Hurry up, before Sister comes looking for you."

"But what shall I do?"

"You know what to do. If you are going to let that big girl hurt you, that's your own fault. Stand up for yourself. If you don't, I'll come over and belt you myself."

I took off flat out, back to my sink, feeling really sad about what Banner had said, especially knowing that she wasn't going to help me. Then on the other hand I took into account that she was going to belt me if I did nothing to Kelly for myself. Sr Birgit had finished scooping out the chocolate mixture into the big cake trays. She left the empty chocolate bowl and spoon on the heap of dirty pots and pans beside me. Quite a lot of mixture remained in the bowl and I suddenly got this thought in my head.

I picked up the bowl and spoon and placed them purposely next to Kelly, who was packing clean dishes away on a shelf next to the sink. Birgit was standing directly opposite us on the other side of the big table, with her back turned to us, keeping an eye on the cakes in the oven. Every now and again she glanced around the kitchen to make sure that all of us were working.

While Sister wasn't looking, I quickly picked up the wooden spoon, scraped up some chocolate mixture, and licked it all off. Kelly saw me.

"Oh waa ... you gunna get into trouble, you not allowed to do that."

"Kelly, Sister Birgit is all right, she not like Sister Gertrude, she'll let you lick the dish, she won't say nothing. If she see you she'll just smile at you. She not really in charge of us, she a new Sister."

I called out to Birgit that I needed to go toilet. She looked over at us, "Vhat do you vant girl ...?" Kelly was licking the dish.

Sister's face turned red. Little did Kelly know Birgit's strange habit of smiling when she got really wild, and the more she got wild, the bigger the smile on her face. Kelly was still licking the dish.

I disappeared out the door to the sound of her cries and the echoing crack of the wooden spoon breaking. Kelly never spoke to me for months after that, but I didn't care. I still had Banner for a mate.

Changing of Duties

I was going on ten years old. The last Sunday of every month we used to have what was called changing of duties. Just before we went to bed that Friday night, Sr Ursula, who was mainly in charge of us, would come into the dormitory with a piece of paper from one of our school pads. With a stern look, she told us to stand up straight in front of her, while she read out our jobs: who would work in the kitchen, who would clean out the bathrooms, and so on.

While Sister continued reading, I stood amongst my mates waiting patiently, feeling pleased because my name wasn't called early. Usually if you were left until last you had something really good lined up for you, like a reward for doing your last job well.

When change of duties came around we used to get happy and stand there smiling. We hung out for the reward of a cake of green Palmolive soap, or a small holy picture, or a small bottle of lavender scent. Sometimes it was hair oil, or a comb, or a couple of boiled lollies.

Sr Ursula called my name, "Glenysen Sprattsen, you did not work well in zer kitchen on your last shob. Sister Gertrude tells me zhat you upset zer younger girls." I put my head down and rubbed the floor with my left foot, while my hands twitched the collar of my dress. I hated being jarred in front of the other girls. Talk about shame.

Her face red as a beetroot and spit flying everywhere, Sister got carried away. Both her hands flung out in different directions, and she muddled up her speech, which was nothing unusual. When she reached that stage we found it hard to control ourselves from laughing, especially if we looked at one another. We couldn't keep a straight face, so I had my head down.

"Oontz anozzer zhing, Glenysen Sprattsen, Sister Gertrude tells me zhat you are ..." She lifted her head in the air, her forefinger tapping her mouth, searching for the right word to describe my behaviour. Banner leant on me, sniggering, and dug my ribs. I nearly choked. I could feel the vibrations in her body.

"Girls," Sr Ursula continued, glancing around at the others, who were all by now smirking, "vhat iss zhis vord? Ah yes, zhis iss zer vord, no? S–i–l–l–y!" She was pleased that she had found her word, but her face soon changed as she looked at me again.

"You are silly in zer kitchen. Sister Gertrude can't vork viz you, oontz all zer ozzer girls, zhey cannot do vork viz you zhere, oontz ... oontz vhen you are to make zer butter, Sister Gertrude finds zer smaller girls turning zer handle and vhere iss Glenysen Sprattsen? Sr Gertrude finds you licking zer chocolate cake bowl oontz vooden spoon, behind zer larder door!

"Oontz for zhis, Glenysen Sprattsen, you are to vork in laundrin. Iss zhis understanding to you, girl?" She finally let her waving arms come to rest beside her body, still clinging to her jobs paper. I looked into her excitable face, which was still red as a beetroot.

"Yes, Sister." All the girls were staring at me.

"Oontz also Glenysen Sprattsen," her face was still red as a beetroot, "you are to be first in line for confession zhis coming Saturday."

I felt really sick in my stomach after hearing Ursie give me that job. I hated working in the old laundry, I got strange vibes from past experiences there. Sr Ursula turned to Banner.

"Oontz Banner, you vis zhese following girls vill vork in laundrin too: Lilly, Poppy, Sally, Zelda and Zhelma. Yah, you vill all vork viz our new Sister. Her name iss Sister Prudence oontz she has not long kommen from Shermany, oontz you vill do pleasing vork to her." I glanced at Banner and the other girls. The gloomy looks on their faces showed they felt the same.

One good thing I thought about before I closed my eyes that night, apart from the new girls who joined us, I'd be working with Banner and my old mates from earlier days, even though we all hated doing the washing.

Watch Out for Sister

That Monday morning, knowing we had to work in the laundry, I didn't feel like eating my breakfast of dry bread soaked in boiled milk, with sugar sprinkled over it. Then came eight o'clock, the time for all the girls to start their jobs.

On our way over we took our time, strolling and talking about the new Sister, wondering if she would be kinder towards us than the other nuns. Then the laundry came into view. The two big wooden doors were swung back either side and Sr Prudence was standing there with her Waterloo boots on. A navy blue apron was strung around her middle over the full, ankle-length navy blue habit that hung down over her chubby frame. Her round face stuck out like the moon under her great veil. Around the face part of the veil was a rim of starched white, which helped keep her hair tucked underneath, so no strands showed.

As we reached the laundry Sr Prudence's piercing blue eyes went right through us and we knew that feeling so well. They all seemed to have this in common, a way of being not easy to understand, not easy to please and very moody. Sister looked at us with an anxious smile on her face while we milled around her, trying to sus her out.

"Good morning, Sister."

"So you all kommen for shob, yah?"

We nodded our heads. "Oontz, vhat iss your name," she pointed at me, and when I told her she started stuttering, trying to pronounce it. "How are you saying zhis name, girl?"

Banner piped up then, as she loved to make us feel shame for fun, and she also got a kick out of ridiculing any new nun. Banner explained all our names real slow-way, ending with mine, "G–l–e–n–y–s–e."

Sister followed the motions of Banner's mouth and after trying for a while became puzzled. "Ve don't have zhis name in Shermany. Lilly, Sally, oontz Zhelma, yes ve have zhese names. Some of our Saints in our church have zhese names also. Banner and Zelda ve also not have zhese names in Shermany." Pleased that she sorted out at least some of our names, she clapped her hands together.

"Komm girls, ve shall do vork, yah?" Sister scurried off to help the big girls lift the clothes out with stirring sticks from two huge coppers, which were built just outside the laundry. We carried the washing into the laundry in old cane baskets for scrubbing on a huge wooden table.

This table stood in the middle of the laundry with circular wooden blocks placed all around it. The brothers had cut them from the old redgums they felled to clear the land for farming. We had to stand on these stepping blocks, because we couldn't reach the table without them.

We each had a bucket of cold water to dip the clothes in. They were still very hot to touch, straight from the copper. Our job was to scrub the clothes with a stiff brush and a piece of soap broken off a bar as long as an arm, called Relax soap. The piece was still awkward to work with because it was so thick and we couldn't hold it properly in our small hands. To break the bar into bits we'd bash it on the edge of the table.

We hated washing and messed around a lot. Banner would start us off. When she saw us trying to break our soap, she'd come along and snatch it out of our hands.

"Gimmie that soap." We never tried to hold it back from her. After a few bangs on the edge of the table she'd have it in bits but instead of just giving it to us she would chuck the pieces into our buckets of water. She'd pelt them in so hard we would get splashed all over. We used to laugh and think it was fun.

When Sr Prudence wasn't around we chucked clothes into Banner's bucket, right in front of her, splashing her all over. We left our soap in the water till it was all mushy and then ducked our faces into the bucket, smearing slimy soap around our mouths and blowing bubbles. We had fun running all over the laundry chasing and trying to pop them. Sr Prudence never saw what was going on. She would send an older girl to check on us, but then we'd be all hard at work scrubbing away and looking weary.

When it was all done we walked around like half-drowned ducks. Then we had to help with the hanging out. I remember on this particular washday, Lilly and I found ourselves right away down along the end of the line going towards the creek. We finished hanging our pile and started walking slowly back.

Halfway back we stopped and took out our gings, the shanghais we carried all the time inside our clothes. We thought we'd shoot up a few crows, because we hated those black birds, always calling out, "Ah-ah-ahhh." After a few shots we continued back toward the laundry but stopped again at the line where the nuns' underwear was flapping and filling with the breeze. The nuns' clothing was hung out on long lines between posts, propped up in the middle by wooden poles. The nuns told us that they were married to God and going to be angels. Us little girls thought their underwear was sacred and we weren't allowed to touch it.

They wore the most peculiar clothes. As we looked at their big Bombay bloomers blowing and flapping in the breeze, we could well understand what part of the body they belonged to, but trying to work out the white bit of material with cords going crisscross fashion down each side and silver clips dangling down at the front and back — that was beyond us.

Another article was a long piece with clips at the end, and yet another that looked like our own singlets. There were long dresses, like our night dresses, and then these things which looked like saucers and had straps all around and clips at the back. We thought it was some kind of shanghai the nuns made.

As we got older we found out that the thing with crisscross cords was a corset to hold their stomachs in and the clips were to keep their stockings up. The things we thought night dresses were petticoats and the shanghais were bras. As for the long piece of material with clips at each end, that went around the nuns' chests, to press the shapes of their breasts flat. Being nuns, they weren't to expose the least part of their bodies to the public.

Lilly stopped and laughed.

"Sprattie, I'll bet you can't hit them bloomers from where I am going to stand." I watched Lilly take a couple of steps away, stoop down, pick up a stone and load her ging.

"Watch out for Sister," she called, as she let fly. She kept zinging away, hitting the nuns' bloomers and putting dirty marks on them. She was running out of ammunition, so I bent down myself to collect some stones for Lilly.

"Ach girls, vhat iss zhis?" Sr Ursula's angry voice startled me out of my wits. She ran up and started flogging into Lilly with open hand slaps. Lilly was crouched holding her hands over her head, crying out "Mummy, Mummy, ouch!"

Every time one of us was hit, we used to sing out for our mums. When I saw my mate copping it, I could do nothing. I stood there with all these stones in my fist and started bawling too. In her mad fury, Sister rushed over. I dropped the stones to put my hands over my head as the same flogging came down on me. When she finished hitting us, we had to stand there sobbing and sniffing while she went mad in her lingo.

"Zhis iss a mortal sin girls, you haf sinned oontz are bad. For your punishment you are to tell Father in confession zhat you destroyed private zhings belonging to zer nuns."

Her fingers plucked at the bunch of keys dangling from the side of her habit, rattling them all the time she spoke.

"Take your hands down from your face girls, and stop zhis

stupid nonsense. Look vhat has happened to zer washing!"

Lilly and I lowered our hands and looked — the great white bloomers were covered with polka-dot mudstains.

Albertus

The monastery was strictly out of bounds to us girls, those were the nuns' orders. Every evening after the fathers and brothers had eaten, we would be cleaning out our big dining room. We'd finished our meal same time as they finished theirs, although they'd have to walk past our dining room windows on the way to the church to say evening prayers.

Albertus was our favourite priest, kind and gentle and usually smiling. He had a round, chubby face and a big red nose, which held up a pair of thick spectacles. He was known to us as Father Superior or Rector, and mainly concentrated on running the place. Now and again we would help him out in his garden. The little girls would go to great pains, sneaking over to the monastery for one of Father's special rewards, when he returned to his room at night.

The wooden windows went right along the length of all the buildings and ended at the dormitory in a brick wall. This was awkward for us when we were watching for Father walking past. We'd dart from one set of windows to another, trying not to make it too obvious to whatever nun was looking after us, as they watched us closely.

Our tables were long and covered with lino and each had two long bench seats beside it. We put one knee up on the bench, then we'd run our rag all the way down, hopping on one leg and one knee, while our eyes concentrated out the window, on Father. Half the time we'd have to explain why we never saw the bench end in front of us, and stumbled or bruised a knee.

We'd continue our duties and by the time Father reached the church we finished our job and Sister would let us go to play in our field, the girls' field, for about an hour before bedtime. Our group of girls would get away from the rest of them and play our own game of hide and seek. Somehow or another, this game would end up at the monastery, near Fr Albertus' bedroom. By this time he would have finished saying prayers, left the church and would be in the sitting room.

Father smoked cigars all day long, his hair was snow-white and his fawny half-mast trousers looked like blown-up bloomers, held onto his big frame by a pair of braces. He wore hobnail boots, and black woollen socks covered most of his legs, so nothing was bare. Sometimes he walked with a thick wooden walking stick.

At night he'd smoke his pipe instead of cigars. Father would be listening to the news on an old wireless, while we'd be perched around like a bunch of starving chooks waiting for him to get up out of his armchair and go to his room. No matter if it was winter or summer we'd wait patiently staring at the brothers reading their German papers or whatever, but all the time watching Father too. Sometimes he would move in his chair to get a better position or cross his legs and we'd all scramble up on the verandah to get ready for the dash to Father's room, only to take our positions on the ground again.

When Father finally came out we'd run behind him to his room where we'd wait patiently in a line while he unlocked a cupboard and took out a flat white box. This had all sorts of marbles in it, from tombowlers, the biggest, to peewees, the smallest and prettiest.

There were never more than one or two peewees, and this was disappointing to the girls because they were so colourful and neat, like miniatures. There were plenty of milkies, catseyes and torn collars. Father's false teeth would click as he asked us girls to speak up loud to let him know what marble we wanted. He was a bit hard of hearing. Sometimes he gave us boiled lollies from a big square tin. When he had handed out to us our reward and we'd all got a marble or a lolly, we'd thank him and say, "Good night Father, may God bless you." As we left his room, he told us not to make so much noise outside while waiting for him, because he couldn't hear the wireless! He must have known we were there all along.

The Only Father I Knew

It was 1958. An extra table had been put in our dining room, down the bottom end, and there was a lot of whispering at breakfast.

"What's Lola and Lynn so happy about? They don't seem to care if Sister Ursula hears them," I said to Florry next to me.

"They don't care even if Sister punishes them."

"Why?"

"Sprattie, haven't you heard? Lola and Lynn's brother is coming today. One of the big working girls told some of the others. There will be more boys coming now."

We finished our semolina. Lola and Lynn had told us about their brother Jimmy, now we were watching them smile away.

"Remember how Lynn used to pray to God at night?" Florry whispered. We knew what she had been praying for. Father often told us in Catechism that if anything bothered us and we needed something, God would answer our prayers.

"Well, He must be solid, because He heard them. Now He's giving them their brother." I glanced over at the empty chairs. "That's why the table is over there, that's where them girls' brother will be sitting."

"Sprattie, why can't we pray to God to give us a brother too?"

"It's a pity we can't see God, otherwise we could go right up to Him and ask Him straight out."

"Sprattie, don't be silly, you know Father and Sister tell us God is a ghost, you have to have trust and believe in him."

"And it won't do us any good, because you and me don't like ghosts, unna?" Little did I know at that very time I had a brother. He was growing up in another Home far away from me and my two sisters, Sally and Nita. I found out about my brother later when I left the home to be a working girl myself.

Lola and Lynn's brother arrived that day to the same sort

of greeting I'd had. Jimmy came from a country town called Ralston. He was collected by the Native Welfare and put in a Boys' Home in Perth until he could be fetched by Father and Brother. We were quite used to these scenes. We all milled around and giggled a lot because his bloomers looked funny and he had the skinniest legs out.

For some of us who had grown from little more than babies in the Home, it was the first time we set eyes on a boy. There was hardly any hair on his head and his big brown-marble eyes looked like they were ready to pop out. He burst out crying. Lola and Lynn both bent down and hugged him close to their bosoms, while Fr Albertus still held on to his hand.

Then Sr Ursula interrupted our circle. Father passed Jimmy over to her and she took his right hand and walked with him to the dining room. We all followed behind Lola, who was clinging onto her brother's left hand for dear life, and Lynn right with her. We were all jumping and running and laughing. It was so funny and strange to have a boy amongst us girls.

One day we were playing a game called ringie. The idea was to draw a big circle in the dirt, into which we'd all chuck whatever marbles we owned. Holding the marble between the thumb and index finger we'd each have our shot and see who could hit the most marbles out of the ring. Anything you hit out you could keep. On this occasion there were four of us playing and before we started our game we made an agreement that we would play for keeps.

Delia was now considered one of us. She was tall, medium build, with black curly hair and used to show off a lot, especially when it came to playing marbles. She thought she was king pin.

I only had four marbles, one of which was a tombowler. So I threw in the three and kept the big tombowler to shoot with. The other girls had about ten each, but I didn't mind that because I was looking forward to adding some more to my own collection. When it came to my turn, there was still a lot in the ring, as the other girls had missed. I took my turn with the tombowler and knocked three out of the ring in the one go!

I was so happy I rushed around whooping and clapping my hands. I was bending down to pick my winnings up and put them in my pocket, when Delia grabbed a marble and would not give it up.

"Delia, give me that marble, I won it, I knocked it out of the ring!"

It was her peewee.

"I made a mistake, I didn't mean to put my favourite in the ring!"

"Too bad, if you don't give it up, I'll punch you in the face." She pushed me and I stumbled over the marbles in the ring. The other girls moved back, they could see I was getting wild. I jumped up and took hold of the front of Delia's dress and was about to punch her in the nose.

"Girls, girls! Vat iss going on?" Sr Ursula was standing there, her red face twitching. She looked really mad. We all knew the signs, the way she was rattling the bunch of keys that hung down from the belt on her habit.

"Glenysen Sprattsen. Komm over here!" I walked over and stood nervously in front of her. My first reaction was to put my hands over my head and cower, because Ursie was very good at hitting, no questions asked. She told the other girls to kneel down where they were standing. At the harshness of her voice they fell down on the gravel, thinking they were going to get a hit too.

Sr Ursula spoke to me in a soft voice. "Girl, your father vas killed today. A vater tank fell off zer back of a truck oontz rolled on him. Vere he vas vorking." I felt a numbing sensation all over my body as we recited after Sr Ursula the prayers for the dead, "May the souls of the faithfully departed through the mercy of God rest in peace, Amen."

After the prayers we girls remained kneeling on the ground. I didn't feel the hard stones under my knees. I was waiting for Ursie to hit me. It all seemed so strange. I wanted to say, "That's my father, over there. He's all right," pointing to Fr Albertus, who was standing over by the buildings in his cassock. He was the only father I knew. Sr Ursula told us to get up and left us wondering why we did not receive punishment.

Delia came over to me and said she didn't want to fight me any more. "Here, Sprattie, you can have it." She handed me the peewee. We all went off with our arms around one another.

My Secret

I recall a stage of my life, about eight or nine years of age, when Poppy and I shared our secrets. Poppy was very close to me. We took one another as sisters, because everything we did, we did together.

We all had something we could cling to and cherish. Something we called our secret. Usually I wouldn't share mine with anybody. The only time I'd show someone my secret was when one of the other girls said hers was better than mine. Now and again we had competitions to see who had the best.

Like this day, Poppy came across me prospecting in the old dump, not far from the old chook yard, which the Italians made in the 1950s. We found out later, they were there before the Germans took over the mission and the Italian nuns must have used this dump to chuck away all their broken crockery and bottles.

"Sprattie what are you doing?"

"I found some bits of pretty glass and broken plates with flowers on and I am collecting them for my secret."

I stood up in front of her and I held my clenched fist out, so she could only see bits sticking out of my hand.

"Open your hand. I can't see the colours properly."

"No, this is all I'm showing you. You want a proper look, show me where your secret is, and what you got in it."

Poppy stood there for a while, rubbing her foot in the dirt, hesitating with her head down, as I waited patiently, rubbing flies from my eyes and rolling them off my face, as they were pretty bad. She finally gave in.

"Okay Sprattie, I'll show you, but promise you won't tell the other girls." Poppy walked off in the direction of the chook yard. I followed behind her, promising not to tell anyone.

Suddenly she stopped right in her tracks. I banged right into her and nearly lost all my treasures. I got a fright thinking she had seen a snake. She grabbed the sleeve of my dress, and pulled me over to her.

"Promise me you won't tell Banner." Still clutching at my treasures, I blessed myself with one hand.

"True God, I won't tell no-one."

The chook yard was just an old building covered in grass with logs all around. We circled round to the front and Poppy went to a clump of bushes and squatted down. I crouched down beside her, emptying my treasures into my dress, and tied a knot in it.

"Sprattie, my secret is here," Poppy took a stick and started scraping the dirt away. "Now you show me yours, hurry up."

"No." I gathered my dress higher and sat back on the ground in my bloomers, crossing my legs. My lips pouted out, I wouldn't give in.

"Oh you'll get into trouble if Sister catch you sitting there like that. You know you're not allowed to show your bloomers."

"I don't care. Hurry up I want to see your secret."

By this time Poppy was cupping the dirt away with her hands, brushing it close behind me as I leaned over, then she came to it.

"There, Sprattie, see?" As I crouched up closer, making sure of a good glimpse at her secret, I saw coloured green paper and red paper, with pieces of bright green glass over it.

"Poppy, that's solid." As quick as she had uncovered it, that's how quick she hid it again.

"Now show me yours, and promise you're not gunna tell them other girls where mine is."

"Nah, I won't. Now hurry up and follow me, otherwise if you're too slow you're not gunna see nothing."

When I got to the post we squatted down and with a stick I scraped away at the dirt till I came to my secret. I lifted off the mauve glass.

"See Poppy here it is!"

I had pieces of crockery and bits of stained glass, spread around the bottom of the hole. She excitedly helped me arrange my treasures, asking me all the time if she could have some. I played deaf making sure that none of the things I had collected was missing. I once had something else that I buried with my treasures. I found it one day with Thelma.

We were out playing in a paddock, which the nuns called playing fields. The field had a slope and down the bottom was one of the beauties of the mission, a big creek, where we spent hours catching tadpoles, when we were given permission to play. That was after our work was done.

We'd find oval-shaped fish tins in the dump and set them afloat in the creek. It was a real thrill chasing behind them. This particular day there was the same old gang of us girls, Sally, Poppy, Florry, Banner, Thelma and myself, all running and splashing in the creek and watching whose tin could go the furthest with the flow of the water before bumping into a log or stick and tipping over.

I was the last in line and Thelma was in front of me. The rest were screaming and shouting ahead but I was too busy concentrating on my tin when, "Oh no," it bumped against what seemed to be a stick.

I stooped down but Thelma distracted me, singing out, "What's wrong?" I lifted my head to say that this horrible stick had stopped my tin, and nearly nose dived into the creek. As I just about kissed the muddy bottom, I realised the object wasn't a stick at all, but a dark green spout protruding from the creek bed.

"Sprattie, get up from there, your tin gone flying that way, look," Thelma sang out. At this stage I'd lost interest in my tin, for I had discovered that there was something attached to the spout and I was scooping the sand away to find out what it was. I called Thelma over in such an excited voice that she tripped as she came running and fell down beside me.

"My glasses!" Thelma blurted out, as she groped around in the muddy water but I ignored her. She could hardly see without her thick glasses.

"Choo, Thelma, look here what I got, I reckon I am solid." I dragged the object out of its hole. There was a powerful sucking noise and a beautiful green china teapot emerged. Dark green, with no patterns on it, and no lid.

"What ...? Oh, look what God gave me!" Shouting at the top of my voice, I forgot about Thelma. The nuns taught us to believe in God. If you were good, they said, God would always reward you. That's what we grew up thinking, so if we found anything, God gave it to us because we were good. I was still too excited to notice Thelma's plight.

"Look here, what this thing? I pulled it up from the mud. I banged my toe on a lump looking for my glasses."

I grabbed the lump from her and sat down to let the water wash the thick mud away from its surface, which was hollow on one side. I was still cradling my teapot in the middle of my dress. Crouched down in the creek I couldn't care less how soaked I was. When I saw that the object was dark green like the teapot, I gripped the teapot in one hand and leapt up.

"It's the lid! Oh look! Thanks, Thelma." I started skipping away, clutching the teapot and its lid.

"Sprattie, find my glasses, I can't see without them, wait for me." She was wading in the water, bending and groping as she searched the muddy bottom. I stopped in my tracks.

"Oh sorry sister girl, I forgot all about you." I took my

jumper off. I didn't feel cold even though it was freezing. I rolled up the teapot and lid in the jumper to make them safe and plunged back into the water. I found her glasses caught between two twigs, dragged them out dripping and gave them to her.

"Hurry up, put them on."

Unwrapping the teapot, I placed it up on higher ground, carefully got out of the water and pranced around my find, clapping my hands and admiring the dark green china, which did not have a scratch on it. I was so thrilled, saying thanks to Thelma for the lid and thanks to God for the pot, when I saw the other girls running towards us like a mob of sheep. I clung to my teapot, feeling uneasy, watching Thelma squinting and jabbering on about it. How she saw it through all the water on her glasses I don't know. There was a commotion as the rest of the girls arrived. They pushed Thelma out of the way.

"Choo, choo Sprattie, where did you get that teapot?" I told them I had dug it out of the creek. They were all grasping for it.

"Could we hold the teapot?"

"No, I'll be right, I can carry it myself." I strutted off, holding tight to my find, leading the procession back to the mission. Later I buried it in my special place, with my secret things, only taking it out to put tadpoles in when I went down the creek, and for playing in our cubby-houses. I was so proud of that teapot!

It was a dark drizzly Sunday afternoon. Sr Ursula said we could stay indoors and play games. Usually we went for a walk, but today Sister left us in the dining room, which we used as a play room on days like this. Banner was sick of playing snakes and ladders, so she made Thelma, Florry, Sally, Poppy and me go with her to catch tadpoles. As our leader, Banner used to make us do all sorts of things. We were petrified about getting into trouble with the nuns, but Banner didn't care. She always seemed to be able to get out of trouble, leaving us to take the blame.

So this particular day, along with the other girls, I followed Banner down to the creek. I was scared and clung to my green teapot. We soon forgot our fears when we saw the running water and tadpoles. I put my teapot down on a bit of a log that was on the verge of the creek and tucked my dress into my bloomers. Soon as I caught a tadpole I ran and put it in my teapot.

Even though Florry was my friend, we squabbled and fought. She was always doing things that upset me, like poking tongue, or trying to find fault. Now she wanted to put her tadpoles in my teapot.

"Go and find your own thing to put your tadpoles in." I dropped a tadpole in and replaced the lid. Then I went off with my nose up in the air, leaving Florry glaring at me.

"My sister found that lid for you, I'm gunna tell her on you and she'll punch you up."

Couple of minutes later, I heard the tinkle of shattering crockery. I turned around in shock and fell on my seat in the water. I saw Florry running flat out towards the mission, and screamed real loud. The cold water shocked me even more. I struggled to my feet and saw my teapot beneath the log all in pieces, and the tadpoles lying listlessly beside it.

I gathered up the pieces, sobbing my heart out. By this time all the other girls were piled around me, wanting to know what happened. To Banner it was a great joke that Florry smashed my teapot. I couldn't understand how she seemed to get real pleasure out of our misfortunes.

I walked to my landmark, the old post, and sat down crying. Sally and Poppy helped me bury the pieces with my secret.

That was the end of the teapot. They put their arms around me and told me not to worry, they'd get Florry for me. We made our way back to the mission sopping wet to face Sr Ursula.

I couldn't have cared less if I was belted, I was too hurt inside to feel any pain. We were all in trouble for going down to the creek, but as usual Banner got out of it and we took the hits. When supper-time came that evening Florry missed out having her soup, because I accidentally bumped it off the table.

Now We Have to Go to Confession

Father Sears was tall, with blond hair and blue eyes. He was a very highly strung person. Every time he got angry his face would go really red and his whole body start to shake. He had the habit of banging his hands together before giving us a hit.

It was during our religious lessons, in the hour before school started, that Fr Sears explained the Ten Commandments. I could understand some like, 'Thou shalt not steal', but not others like, 'Thou shalt love thy neighbour as thyself'. Fr Sears explained.

"You've got to love your enemies as well."

I thought that was impossible — how could I love Florry? She's always being horrible. How can I put my arms around her and love her if she hits me? She broke my teapot. My first thought would be to strangle her.

Then there was the way Fr Albertus dealt with us. All the years at the mission while we were growing up, I couldn't understand him. I couldn't understand the nuns either. They acted every day like they were angels and yet every Saturday afternoon when we were all in church waiting to go into the confession box, they were lined up first in front of us.

The sisters brought us up so very strict that we weren't allowed to do anything. I found it difficult going to confession. Most of the time we told lies, so we had something to tell the priest.

On this particular Sunday afternoon we were on one of our walks in the bush. Banner, Sally, Florry, Thelma, Lynn, Poppy, Zelda and I were all together, including some newcomers to our fold, Jackie and Maria. In our little group we all raced ahead of Sister, running and seeing who could jump over the most logs.

We came out to a clearing near this paddock where bulls and cows were grazing. Banner sang out to all the girls to come over near the fence and line up. Wondering what she wanted us for, we all ran over, grabbed the fence and started swinging on it. We had a habit of teasing cows and bulls whenever we were near them.

So we started singing out "Mooooooo... mooooooo..." And they all looked at us, shaking their heads, ready to charge. Banner shouted, "Keep quiet and get off the fence." She gave it one of her manly shakes, and one by one we all fell and hit the ground.

"Get up, you girls and come here. Quick, stand up!"

We all jumped up in fright, thinking it must be a dingo out in the paddock causing this uneasiness amongst the cattle as they were all fidgety and mooing. I stood quietly beside Banner.

"Sprattie, you see that big black bull on top of that cow?"

"Yes, Banner, what are they doing?"

"That bull should walk itself instead of asking the poor cow for a piggyback. Unna, you girls?" All the other girls agreed and I felt sorry for that cow. In our play we mission girls gave one another piggybacks all around the place. We gazed at the poor cow feeling sorry for it. We'd get upset if we ever saw any animals getting hurt.

"Gurn, get away from her. Gurn get, get." Lynn picked up a stone and chucked it at the bull. We all joined in this except Banner.

"That's enough, girls. Sprattie, when you go to confession next Saturday, you are to tell Father Albertus that you saw this bull making the cow give it a piggyback in the paddock!"

Nothing more was said until the following weekend. Saturday afternoon I was really proud that I had something to report to Father. When it finally came to be my turn, I marched into the confessional box feeling reverent and pious. I knelt down, blessed myself and began.

"Bless me Father, for I have sinned."

"Go on, child, what are your sins?" I was so anxious that I

stuttered out how I had seen this bull on top of this cow in the paddock the other day.

"What were they doing, child?"

"I don't know, Father, but it looked like the cow was giving that bull a piggyback!"

There was a pause, then Father spoke, "These are your penances, child. You will go out now and say ten Hail Marys and ten Our Fathers." I blessed myself and on my way out, Banner looked at me. When her turn came she wasn't in for long. She walked past me with a smile as I stood there saying my penance and asking God for forgiveness.

One of my pleasures when growing up in the mission was swimming in our dam, the one especially reserved for girls. On this particular day Banner was our main actor as usual. She, Thelma, Zelda, Sally, Jackie and I had to clean out the drains all round the mission. Did we hate that job!

I thought Sr Ursula gave us all the dirty jobs because she hated us. And my feelings were mutual for her too. I was getting older and starting to think differently about some of the nuns. It did seem that every time the unpleasant jobs came up, I was on the top of the list. To clean the drains we paired off. Zelda and Thelma were given the smaller drain at the back of the nuns' convent and the rest of us girls had the big double drains at the rear of the kitchen.

Whenever Thelma went with Zelda she became real spiteful and thought she was somebody above the rest of us. Zelda was a goodie-goodie and we called her Tell-tale Tit because she always pimped on us. What hurt our group most was seeing Thelma with her. We considered Thelma our sister because she had been with us since the earliest years at the mission.

Zelda had come later on, and she was no fun.

Once she tried to talk to me. I walked right up to her in a hate-full mood, put my face right up close to hers and just about kissed her. I screwed my face, poked my tongue, walked off and left her singing out threats, "Oh waa ... I'm gunna tell Sister on you." I couldn't be bothered looking back. The way I was feeling, if I had looked back, I would have run up, given her an uppercut and dropped her right where she was standing.

While those two were walking away, the rest of us sat with our backs to a fence near our drain, staring at them. We weren't worried about cleaning the drain, we were still having our hate session.

"Have a guess who'll be doing the cleaning?" Banner taunted.

"Thelma will!" We all crowed in a singsong voice and Jackie called to Thelma, "Gurn, you think you solid, but you open, poor thing!"

"Let's hurry up and get these stinkin' drains done," Banner ordered, "then we can sneak down to the dam and have a swim." So we forgot them and got stuck into our drains. We lifted the wooden planks. The smell from the big double drains was so putrid I nearly vomited. We used old jam tins to scoop out the scum and maggots till the drains were empty, then washed them out with hot water and Dettol. It took us two hours to get them clean. By this time we were covered in the muck ourselves and stank horribly.

Just as we dropped the big heavy lids back on, Sr Ursula came along with Lola, the working girl, and gave us our usual dressing down.

"Girls, iss zhis shob finished?"

"Yes, Sister."

"Zhen who told you to shut zer lid down vizout coming to let me know you are finished?"

The normal thing with every job we completed was to report to one of the nuns so it could be inspected and passed. But Sister never bothered to check the drains. I think the smell of us was making her sick. She turned from the drain to us in disgust and started to rattle her bunch of keys, raising herself up on her tiptoes and down again, and up again and down again in a regular motion. "I vill leave Lola in sharge viz you. Lola, you vill scrub zer girls viz scrubbing brush and you vill use plenty of sand soap, yah?"

With that she brought the heels of her black lace-up shoes down hard, clicked them together and marched off, leaving us with the sickening prospect of Lola as supervisor. We made our way to the bathroom, wondering how to escape to the dam for that swim. "I'll think of something," Banner said.

"What if we let Lola scrub us," I pipped in, "and when we are clean ask Ursie if we can go down to the old tree and pick gum." They all knew what I had in mind. The gumtree was not far from our girls' dam.

It really hurt being nice to Lola but we did everything she asked of us. As she scrubbed away I thought, "What if Ursie does allow us to go down to the gumtree and Lola comes with us? If she does, I'll catch her for scrubbing my elbows too hard."

When we were all clean and in fresh khaki dresses with their rick-rack hems, we all trooped down to the convent. We were only supposed to go there to help the nuns wash dishes or during retreats, or for special permission to go anywhere, say for walks or to get gum.

Sister was cleaning out the chapel in the convent, so Banner pushed Zelda ahead and told her to ask permission for all of us, seeing that she was the cheeky one. We waited outside on the verandah stairs. Next minute, out comes Zelda with Sr Ursula. We jumped up into a row so Sister could see how clean we were. She looked us over like a hawk stalking over her prey.

"Zhis iss better how you look zhis time, girls. You vant to go to zer gumtree. Ah, first you vill go and have dinner, zhen you must all do your vork and zhen I vill see if you go to zer gumtree, yes?"

60

The door shut behind us. We walked away uncertain about everything. Banner started to mimic Sister and we burst out laughing, even Zelda. All the way to the dining room we recited, "Girls vill haf dinner first!"

Our meal and prayers were over. Finally we were given permission. Free at last, we all ran down the pad behind the dump, through the bush and paddock. We saw the dam but headed straight for the gumtree. When we reached there we took a breather and looked back to make sure the coast was clear, as we could quite easily see the nuns' convent from the dam. Lola came with us, but she was too engrossed in a big lump of gum she had spotted up near the top of the tree. We left her with it and bolted for the dam.

In we went, dresses and all on. We splashed and shouted with joy. Amidst our screaming and laughing Jackie sang out "Baalay — Sister coming." We scrambled out terrified and ran around the high bank of the dam to hide. There we fell in the tall grass, dripping with water.

"Ma-ake-up! Sister not coming." The look on Banner's face when Jackie sang out. We thought she was going to strangle Jackie, when suddenly another girl called across.

"Hey look what I found." It was Zelda. She must have panicked with us and hit the grass when she heard Jackie shout that Sister was coming over. She was holding up these bright coloured bits of clothing made out of a bubbly sort of material, pleated up tight to make it look bubbly.

They belonged to the big working girls, who used to hide them in the grass for use whenever they sneaked away from the nuns to have a swim. Lola snatched them out of Zelda's hands, telling us they were bathers. We had never seen bathers before, let alone knowing how to wear them. Lola put on a pair, making us promise not to tell Sister about the big girls sneaking away to the dam for swims, and hiding their bathers in the grass. We all had a giggling fit about the bathers, she looked so funny because they were too big.

I didn't mind Lola when she joined us girls in a bit of fun. I hated her when she acted like the nuns and pimped on us. Especially when I used to see her in church praying, she looked so reverent that I used to just crack up watching her. Talk about winyarn. After our solemn promise to Lola about the bathers, Banner told her that if she ever pimped on us about anything again, then she would turn around and tell on her too, big girl or not.

"Hey, how many are there?" Banner asked. "We could all have a pair and hang our wet clothes on the grass here to dry, so Sister Ursula won't know we had a swim." It was the first time Lola ever agreed with us. She even said she could do with a swim too, as she chucked a pair to each girl, saying she wouldn't tell on us.

We each picked a separate clump of grass to hide behind and struggled into these bathers on our own. The nuns told us we weren't to show our private parts to anyone. That was a mortal sin. If anyone ever saw our bare bottoms God would punish us because that would be a sin on our part. We'd get real bashful changing in front of one another. Even in bathers we felt half naked, after the baggy dresses.

Jackie came out from behind her grass wearing mauve bathers and strutting like a peacock. We all cracked up — she still had her Bombay bloomers on underneath. Sally went over to her wild.

"Can't you get anything right? You're real stupid. You make me sick." We all kept on laughing and she turned to us.

"Keep quiet!" On Sally went, grumbling at Jackie, knocking her ego down, "When you put bathers on you have to take your bloomers off, like me, see?" Now Jackie was getting mad at Sally.

"Gurn, you not the boss of me, you're winyarn. Unna, you fullas?"

"Choo, you are both solid," Banner told them and she ran off laughing. "Last one in the water the devil going to get you."

I joined in with the girls, splashing and playing around, and then took a spell on the bank. As I flopped down hard I screamed in pain. A big stone had grazed my bottom. The girls gathered round.

"Where'd you get hurt?" I showed them, my bottom in the air, rubbing it like mad. Suddenly Lola was telling the girls to kneel and start praying to God, to ask forgiveness. Then she grabbed my bathers and kept hanging on to the seat of them, shouting to the girls, "Don't look at her any more! Banner, go along the fence and grab a bit of wire." This terrified me because I still felt a sharp pain.

"Sally, how deep did I cut myself?"

I felt like a skinned rabbit on a hook, the way she was holding me up. Banner came back with a twitch of wire and chucked it to Lola, who told her to join the girls in praying on their knees for me. She was using the wire on my bathers now.

"God will heal my sore up, unna Lola?" I whimpered.

"You start praying too, Sprattie. I got something bad to tell you," she said to me. "Stop crying. It's nothing to do with your cut. You got one big hole in your bather britches, and we all seen your backside. That's why I am fixing it up with wire. How do you think us girls feel? Now we will all have to go to confession, because of you!"

Don't Cry You Fullas

In the early 1960s there were heaps more girls and boys at Wandering, being brought up the good Christian way.

One night our gang was on Sally's bed telling our usual ghostie yarns by the flickering light of the lantern. We were joined by a couple of newcomers to the fold, Nicky and Bella. As was often the case with arrivals, they were sisters.

I would get terrible cramps on the bed because there just wasn't any room to stretch out. We were packed like sardines in a tin, especially for a ghostie yarn. One girl would move, or someone would touch you from behind and sing out baalay! And we'd all tumble together. We were pretty good at acrobatics.

That particular night Nicky and Bella were telling us a ghost story about their mother, an uncle and older cousin. They had lived on a reserve just outside Boolaring, not far from the mission. This older cousin of theirs had an army coat, which he treasured. Rain or shine, freezing or boiling hot, Clinton would wear his coat.

"Cos Clinton found it scrounging in the tip with Mum, Aunty Sissy and our little brothers and sisters, unna, Nicky?" Bella turned to Nicky.

"Yeah, you fullas, them wadjalas chuck out some solid things in the dump, plates, pots and pans and matteress, we got at home, they deadly unna?"

"Choo, wish we was there, we'd clean that dump right out," we said. Bella continued with her story.

"One day Mum ran out of flour to make damper. 'Clinton,' she said, 'go down to Uncle Clive's camp and ask him for a couple of bob. He should have it because he done all that work for that wadjala, picking wool from dead sheep. Hurry up and get him first, before he buy some of that sly plonk from that wadjala Wino Jim. He'll be along soon, it's early in the morning. Quick now, hurry up. Tell him I might wander down that way myself later and have a yarn with him.'

"Clinton put this big army coat on, thinking he was solid, and you fullas should see that bike he found in the dump. Cos he thought he was moorditj, taking off to town on his bike and his big coat was fairly flying in the breeze."

"Was the bike deadly?" we pipped in. Bella threw her hands up and killed herself laughing.

"Sis, tell these fullas about Clinton's bike." Nicky was laughing too. "Proper winyarn," she blurted out, describing how she could still see that rusty frame wobbling off into the distance.

"Clinton never came back all day," said Bella. Their mother had told them he met a yorga, whom he was mardong for, so he forgot about the bag of flour. We didn't know what Bella meant by mardong. We knew that yorgas were girls.

"What's mardong?"

"Tell Sprattie what it means, Nicky, you should know what mardong means. Who's that pretty kid you met at Boolaring pool?"

Nicky went shame.

"Gurn Bella, don't be silly, who want that dopey-looking thing." We all laughed, as Bella went on to say how her cousin was sweet on this yorga, and there was her mother getting worried.

"She walked around the camp saying, 'Girls, I wish Clinton would hurry up, I'm waiting to cook, I wonder what could have held him up?' Uncle Allan was there at the time and he said, 'Stop worrying, Maun,' which was short for Maureen, 'you know what Clinton's like when it comes to womens. He must be kissing the lips off her by now.' Mum was getting wild. 'Stop talking like that, Allan, you ought to be ashamed of yourself, he's your son, your own flesh and blood.'

"Uncle Allan used to like teasing Mum. He got up teasing-way and dug her in the ribs.

'Cos he's my son, Maun, can't you see? He's taking after his father.'

'Huh, then I pity the poor kid.'

"She sat down on the camp bed, worried because it was getting dark now. She lit up the kerosene lamp and hung it on a pole in the tent and got herself ready to go to bed, since there was nothing else to do. 'Come on you girls, get a wash. Uncle Allan, fill up the tub for them, and then you all get to bed. I don't know what happened to your cousin Clinton but I'll murder the scoundrel when I get my mits on him.'

"Just as well Uncle Allan had some spare bread to feed us. So we got our wash and scrambled into bed, me up one end, Nicky down the other, and Mum blew out the flame of the lantern, then went outside to sit by the campfire that Uncle lit for her. They were just yarning away and listening to all the other Nyungars, our relations, talking and laughing, and I don't know what time Mum came to bed.

"We woke up to Mum screaming. She was trying to quieten Clinton. He was a sight in the middle of Mum's bed. He had no coat, his hair was sticking up straight and he looked real sick. His normal colour is real black but he looked like he'd changed it. The moonlight on his face showed white, ay? We thought he was dead."

We all pressed in closer to Bella, as we were starting to get shivers down our spine. The flame in our lantern flickered as a sudden gust of wind rattled the window panes and sent a howl down the chimney. We clung tighter to one another.

"Hey, I am getting frightened you girls! You want me to keep on talking, or shall I finish it tomorrow when it's daylight?"

"No go on, sis, tell them what happened. You girls aren't frightened, are you girls?"

"Nah. Come on Bella, tell us what happened, we're not frightened." Jackie hit my arms away from her neck. I was nearly choking her.

"All right. Poor Mummy, unna Nicky?" Bella went on. "She was panicking, and crying-way she said, 'You two girls go down the bottom camp and round up your aunties Mabel and Sissy, and go get Uncle Allan and your cousins. Hurry up, get anyone and tell them please hurry because your cousin Clinton is dying. Get Uncle Jack too, he's the medicine man.'

'Shall we send for the doctor in town?'

'No we don't want no wadjala, he'll probably end up giving Clinton poison. They are a bit funny when it comes to looking after blackfellas. We got our own doctors; I'll tell you about that a bit later on girl, when you are older. Now run, quick.'

"We just ran flat out, because we'd seen Clinton lying there jibbering about the graveyard. He did not have his big coat and his old bike was nowhere to be seen. It only took us a little while and we just about had the whole reserve there. Uncle Jack the medicine man was the last to come. Aunty Mabel and Aunty Sissy were holding Clinton and Mummy together and swaying with them, crying at the same time. In came Uncle Jack.

'Keep quiet everybody, stop your crying and go and wait outside. You too, Maureen. He'll be right. Sissy, take the old girl down to your camp and give her some tea. And the kids.'

"Aunty Sissy rounded us all up and we went with her. When we got to her camp she said, 'You girls crawl into that matteress on the ground with your little cousin Billy; I'll attend to your mum.' When we woke up we were still in Aunty Sissy's tent. We came to our senses about what happened that night. Everyone was gone, even Billy. We got up and ran back to Mum, wondering if Clinton had died. Mum was crying and laughing. Cousin Clinton was sitting up smiling. Everyone was still there from that night. Dazed, we ran in and gave Mum and Clinton a big hug each as they grabbed us. We sat on each of their laps, me on Clinton's. You fullas, we didn't know what was going on.

"I turned to Clinton and asked him, 'What happened? We thought you was dying last night.' He wiped the tears from his eyes, 'Never you mind girl, I thought I was dead myself. Take a look on the ground over there.' He was still choked up laughing. Nicky and I jumped off their laps and ran towards a shade tree. There we saw Clinton's bike, smashed properly, with his great army coat stuck through the wheel and all twisted up. Wondering what had happened, we ran back to ask Clinton."

At this moment in the story, first Nicky and then Bella started laughing uncontrollably. All of us on the bed were leaning over one another waiting anxiously.

"Stop laughing you two and tell us what's so funny." So they both pulled themselves together and Bella went on.

"Okay you fullas, I'll try not to laugh again. Well this is what our cousin said happened to him. While he was in town he was with his yorga. He spent Mummy's shillings on that yorga, hey Nicky? They went and bought a tin of camp pie and a loaf of bread."

"Mum was mad with him for that," Nicky broke in. "She hit him with a broomstick across the back because he never thought about us kids back home starving. He was down the river all day, feeding that yorga. Mum sang out to him, 'Choo, she must be a cruel woman. And you Clinton baby, you must be solid. Hey that flame must be fairly burning high for her.' Clinton said to her bashful-way, because we were all listening, 'Shut up, Maun, don't talk in front of the kids like that.'

"Anyway, Clinton didn't realise it was so late, so to get

home quicker, he took a short cut through the cemetery. Now Clinton never liked the graveyard, all our people hated going near it. Mum told us that there were a lot of spirits and devils there and it was haunted.

"Clinton put on this brave act and was fairly wobbling past these gravestones, when all of a sudden he felt this thing pull on his coat. He tried to keep pedalling but nothing was happening. That's when he up with everything and bolted. He got such a shock he just about fainted. And you know what had happened?"

All of us girls were eagerly waiting.

"That solid army coat of his. Well that got stuck in the back wheel of his winyarn bike. He thought the devil had him."

We burst out laughing. Bella and Nicky let out long sighs, "Oh I wish we were home, we miss our home and Mum and Uncle and Clinton."

Suddenly Bella's sighs turned into great big sobs. Nicky grabbed her, with tears falling too and we all stopped laughing. We thought Bella was in pain.

"What the matter you fullas?" We all made a fuss of them, "What wrong, you want me to go and wake Sister in the convent to give you a tablet?"

"No no no," they were shaking their heads, "we want to go back home again."

Of course, Banner, Zelda, Sally, myself and the rest of our gang started feeling sorry and put our arms around them.

"Don't cry you fullas, you'll make us all cry." All the years we grew up in the mission, anytime a kid was hurt or sad, we'd feel their hurt and sorrow with them, especially when it happened to one of our gang.

"I can't stop crying. I miss Clinton and I miss Uncle and Mum so much," Bella blurted out, wiping her eyes with her pyjama top. "I wonder what they are doing now sis?" Nicky grabbed her hand and squeezed it.

"Sis, let's run away from here."

"Choo, we'll all get into trouble."

"I couldn't care less if I do get belted, that's nothing, the sting fades after a while but this kind of pain I am feeling will never go away until I am back home with Mum."

We could see she was getting restless, folding her arms and bending over and rocking where she was sitting on the bed, with knees folded under her arms and pressed into her stomach. Nicky hugged her and gave sisterly strokes to her hair, and then she asked us, "How about it? Do you want to come with us to our home? Mummy and Clinton and all that mob on the reserve will look after yous. Some of that mob might be your relations."

We all looked at her dumbfounded as she went on, "Unna sis, sit up and tell these fullas. Come up, stop crying and tell them." Still sniffing, Bella raised herself up and pulled the sleeve of her pyjama top till it hung loosely and she had something to wipe her nose with.

"Me, Zelda and Thelma will come with you," Banner spoke up.

Taken by surprise at this outburst, Zelda and Thelma agreed, "Yes, we'll come." Zelda saw the shocked look on my face when I heard her say yes. Faithful Zelda, who'd never do anything wrong, I thought she'd be the last person to get in on the act. Bella glanced my way.

"What about the rest of you girls, Sprattie, you coming?"

"Nah, this is my home."

Then Bella put her hands on my shoulders and looked straight at me. "This is not your home." She shook me.

"Where's your mum, Sprattie?"

"She wakes us up every morning."

I noticed tears welling in Bella's eyes again as she put her arms around me and pressed me into her bosom. Everyone just sat there quietly. I felt the back of my head getting wet.

"Bella, you're wetting me."

She gently dabbed my head with her pyjama top.

"Sprattie, I am crying for you."

The Runaways

The following night I stirred when I felt Banner and Thelma each give me a kiss on the forehead. I pretended to be asleep, as I had a notion the girls would come and check on us, just to see if we had changed our minds about going. Besides, I felt that I was in my home already, although in another sense I wouldn't have minded going with the mob. I heard Nicky say, "Banner, leave the little ones. They'll probably get tired with walking. Come on, you fullas." Then I fell asleep.

"Sprattie, Sprattie, quick, wake up, wake up."

Lynn was tugging at my pyjamas. I sat up still half dazed. It was morning. "Banner and Zelda and Thelma and them two other girls Bella and Nicky, they run away. Did you hear them go last night? I was awake, they wanted me to go, but I told them I didn't want to leave you. They made me promise not to tell the nuns on them."

I came to my senses then. By this time, most of us were awake, as the dormitory hummed with everyone talking about the girls who had cleared out.

"Do the nuns know yet, Lynn?"

"Yeah, Lola went down the convent and reported them. Sprattie, I tried to wake you up but you were sound asleep."

"I thought I felt somebody touching me."

"That was Banner mob saying goodbye to you." I looked at all the girls sitting around talking. It seemed funny Banner and Zelda and Thelma not being there.

"Baalay! Sister coming, Sister coming, sh–sh–sh– be quiet." Bodies were darting everywhere, back to their beds. If ever you woke up early in the morning you were not allowed to talk or get out of bed. You were not allowed to go to one another's beds, either. If caught, you would be punished. They made you go to early mass with the nuns and brothers. So we all laid back down again.

We didn't have to wait long. The key rattled in the padlock and Sr Ursula stormed in. We dragged ourselves out to the loud piercing noise of the handbell. Sister's mood could be felt in her vigorous shakes and manner towards us. She went around as usual pulling blankets off the girls who were slow at getting up. We all knelt down and waited beside our beds for the usual prayer, to thank God for a good night's sleep. We remained calm while Sister marched past us up one aisle and down the other.

"Girls, I know vhat vent on here last night, in zer dormitory. Vhy vasn't I told vhat vas going on straight away? You all must know by now, zhis iss a serious matter, oontz you must all expect to be punished!"

"Brozher Edward and Fazher Albertus have gone to look for zer girls. Vhen zhey are found oontz returned to zer mission, you are not to talk to zhem. Zhey vill be locked up in zer Dispensary all day for zheir punishment. Zhen, for zer rest of zer week, you vill join in vis zhem! Oontz for your punishment, you vill vork double around zer place. Zhere vill be no playing in zer field after school. You vill report to me in zer dining room, vhere you vill get your orders to work. Do I make myself understood?!!"

"Yes, Sister."

"Now, ve vill start zer prayers."

We all got up from prayers in silence and continued on with our normal duties. Again it seemed strange not having Banner and Thelma around and I felt sad making my bed. Although Zelda was bossy, I still missed her too. While sitting in school that morning, none of us could relax, wondering about the girls. We sneaked looks out of the school windows to see if there was any sign, like a car coming up, but nothing unusual happened. The louvres were made of stippled glass, so you could not see through them unless they were opened.

Just before dinner time Sr Petra made us stand out in the front of the class to read *Little Red Riding Hood.* After my turn, I walked slowly down the aisle. I was about to sit down when something made me glance again through the open louvres. There was dust coming down the road.

"The ute!" I whispered to Jackie. We didn't get much chance of conversation, we were both startled by the slamming shut of the louvres. Sr Petra left only a few right at the top open, far above our eye level.

Then Sister pulled Jackie and me out of our desks by the ears, and with her fingernails piercing our earlobes, we went screaming either side of her down the aisle. We fell in a bundle in front of the other girls waiting for their turn to read.

"You vill continue reading *Jack and zer Beanstalk!*"

The next week was spent making sauerkraut, with the runaway girls. That was our punishment. There was an old shed built of corrugated iron, with a cement floor. Under the floor was the cellar, where the priests stored the altar wine. The shed had a big iron bar across the door and a padlock. Stairs led up to a top floor, which was also of cement.

All day, barefooted on the cement, we cut up cabbages and put them in six old barrels that were stored there in a row. We couldn't talk much about the running away business because two nuns supervised us. We took it in turns cutting the cabbages or carrying away the outer leaves in iron tubs, for the cows. Along the fence the cows were lined up mooing and chucking their cudded heads in the air, when they saw us coming with a feed for them.

If we tried to talk to one another, the nuns came from nowhere and told us off. Even carrying the cabbage leaves to the paddock, we'd have another nun coming at the back of us, as we'd go along the line feeding the cows.

The runaway girls finally got their chance to tell us their

story, after lights out, sitting on Banner's bed. Lynn started them off.

"Which way you girls go, when you jumped out the window?"

"We headed for the shrine and snuck through the fence at the back and went up in the hills where all them caves are." Sally leaned towards Banner.

"How did yous feel when yous walked past them caves?"

"We were packing it. I never been out walking in the dark before, especially up in the hills."

"Yeah, remember how the big girls keep telling us them hills and caves are haunted? It's a wonder yous didn't see redeyes looking at you from the caves."

"We was trying not to think about that when we went past the shrine," Bella went on. "Banner and us blessed ourselves. All we was worried about was seeing Mum and all of them lot back home again. We got past them caves. Lucky it was moonlight and we could see where we was going. We headed down towards the gully, you know where we pick all them Donkey orchids for the church, when the wildflowers are out?"

"But we was still scared."

Banner gave out a laugh. Bella and Nicky joined in. "Oh, choo Banner, don't girl, we thought we was finished." They both chucked their heads back laughing.

"Shut up yous now," Banner suddenly whispered out loud, "one of those other girls might hear us and go and tell, then we'll all be laughing, sitting up in that scarey old laundry. You know what Ursie is like, she's the main one for locking doors behind us, so be quiet all of you. Now where was I?"

"You was just about to tell us when yous was walking steady-way in the gully."

"Oh yes that's right." Banner picked up her pillow and laid it across her lap, sitting cross-legged. "Righto, I'll try not to laugh. Well I took the lead down this path, you know that one we all follow which leads us out to the quarry. I was walking good-way, and these two here," she pointed to Bella and Nicky, "the main actors, they said to me, 'Banner, we'll take the lead, we're not frightened. Tomorrow we'll be with Mummy and you'll meet all our other relations.'

"'Okay,' I said. So Nicky got in the front, then Bella and Zelda, then Thelma at the back of Zelda and I was last. I was cruel frightened, I had this feeling someone was at the back of me, I am sure I heard footsteps. You know how someone treads on a stick and it makes that cracking noise?"

"Yeah," Bella and Nicky said seriously, "Banner, you know, we'd been hearing them noises all the time too but we didn't want to say anything, thinking you might of got frightened and took off back to the mission."

"No way you fullas, you'd never catch me going back all alone, it was bad enough out there that night with yous three. I wouldn't let go of Thelma, I was hanging on cruel to her dress, hey Thelma?"

"Don't you make me weak Banner," Thelma smiled, "I felt like punching you, cos you was holding me back."

"Bella you was doing the same to me," Nicky murmured as they all had a silent chuckle.

"Anyway, we kept on walking, holding on to one another, trying hard not to show that we was frightened. I think we all had the same thought, 'Ghosts', but none of us would let on. Every now and then someone would whisper:

'Did you hear that noise?'

'Stop shh, what's that?'

'Oh that nothing, don't worry yous, we'll be all right just keep walking.'

"Thelma started complaining she was getting tired. Us girls made out we never heard her. Unna Thelma?" Banner gave Thelma a friendly hit on the back.

"Yeah Banner, I know you all over, I knew you heard me."

"We kept walking, not saying anything until all of a sudden Nicky stopped dead in her tracks. Of course us coming at the back of her banged into her and nearly sent her flying.

'Zelda, look,' Nicky whispered aloud.

'What Nicky, what?' We was just about goonaring ourselves, as we clung to Nicky, breathing all over her shoulder.

'Look up there, standing in the middle of the pad.'

"We looked in the direction her finger was pointing. Then we saw this figure standing up, straight ahead, and we all had the same thought, to take off into the bush. We turned around at once, to start running, but we banged into one another and kept falling over, because every time one of us got up to run, another would pull them down again. There was sand and dust flying everywhere. You girls should of seen us."

By this time we all had our own pillows and were laughing into them. Banner rolled over on her side and couldn't speak. Thelma took up the story.

"We all wetted and puffed ourselves out. Then that strange figure we was trying to get away from suddenly bend down and hopped away in the bushes. We just sat there, silly-way as Banner got Nicky's pillow case with all our fullas' change of clothes in. We got rid of our torn dresses in the bush and looked at one another, and we busted out laughing again. Us girls had aches in our side from laughing. That kangaroo just look like a man, he put the wind up us, hey?"

"Where did you fullas sleep?"

"After that fright, and after we got dressed," Banner spoke again, "I told Nicky to pick our ripped clothes off the bushes, where we chucked them. I explained to these fullas that we'll go to the quarry to sleep on them flat rocks." At picnics we used to lay on our backs on the quarry rocks and watch eagles and chicken hawks soaring in the sky, after bunny rabbits.

"We weren't far from the quarry. I kept pushing these fullas to walk. They wanted to lay down on the ground there, right where we got that fright."

"Don't. We were all cruel tired, our legs felt like jelly."

"Choo Nicky, my legs felt wobbly too but I was trying not to think about it."

Thelma said that her eyes were getting so heavy she couldn't care less. "If I'd seen another kangaroo I'd have fallen to the ground stiff-way and let it jump right over me. I would have just laid there."

"These fullas kept on grumbling, saying to me, 'Banner let's stop here, we'll never get to the quarry.' I didn't take any notice, I just kept on walking weak-way, till it seemed like we were going for hours."

"When we go down that same track from the mission by day, we get to the quarry in no time," Bella spoke up. "We got to that flat rock and our legs gave way, we flopped down and lay together in a bunch, we never even waited to spread our ripped clothes out so we could lay on them. The clothes just stayed where we dropped them beside us. We woke up next morning with the sun shining down on us, burning our faces. We all wondered where we was for a moment, hey Banner?"

"Yeah, it seemed funny, unna you girls, not seeing old Ursie's face glaring at you, and not hearing that bell ringing flat out in your ear." Banner looked at us other girls who had not gone, in a sad kind of way, "You ask Zelda and Thelma, they can tell you the same. It was so peaceful waking up in the bush, listening to the birds, all them different kind of noises they were making, even that old crow cawing away didn't sound so bad."

Nicky said that she felt like she was in a new home. "That's what it's like at our place, we wake up in the bush every morning." Bella agreed. "The bush is our home, you girls, this is what we miss so much at the mission."

"Unna?" Being used to dormitory living, I couldn't understand what she meant.

"When you find your real home one day, Sprattie, I hope you think of me. Then you'll know what I have been trying all along to tell you," Bella went on. "I'll excuse you because you are only little and don't know any better."

I just shrugged my shoulders and leaned closer to Banner, who continued her story. "Everything was going good. We all stood up and stretched and had the biggest yawn out. We held up our arms and with our faces up to the sky we opened our mouths wide, not caring what went in them. We could have had any one of those beautiful butterflies for breakfast. We just let the fresh air and peaceful feeling float in our bodies.

"Then we all went down to that spring for a drink, you remember, further down in the quarry, all us girls found that time, when we was picking ferns for the nuns' convent chapel?" We were all trying to rack our brains which spring this was, because there were springs all round the quarry. "The one closest to that flat rock."

"Oh yeah – just down between them two really big rocks."

Bella took up the story, "That's the one, we soaked our heads in the water too, because Banner said it was cooler for us to walk soakin' wet. We started to feel hungry. Further up the track we found all these wattle trees so we picked a heap of gum and ate that as we walked along. We must have walked for miles. The sun dried our hair and we started getting hot. Nicky said that we shouldn't be far now, hey sis?"

Now it was Nicky's turn, "When we come out to a clearing, we seemed to have left the bush far behind us. We come to this paddock, fenced right round as far as we could see. Far off was a roof of a farmhouse. We just stood there, leaning on the fence. We was happy but we didn't know what to do."

Banner went on.

"These other four girls got through the fence and started bolting for the farmhouse. I went after them flat out. 'Wait you fullas, if we go there them white people might pimp on us.'"

Banner looked over at her mates, "Big shots, these four here." Thelma, Bella and Nicky turned their heads aside, shame-way.

"We couldn't help it, we sorry anyway," Zelda spoke up.

"Too late now to be sorry, we're back here from where we started. These four main actors here, all they thought about was their stomachs. While we was standing there working out whether to go down to the farm or keep walking, Bella and Nicky was saying, 'Banner, they will probably help us, we'll just tell them we got lost while we come this way with our mum and dad from Boolaring, looking for wood. You never know, they might even take us back to the reserve.'"

Banner looked disgusted, "Me feeling hungry too, we flew down that paddock to the farmhouse. We didn't think the farm was so far! Don't know how many gullies we crossed. All the time I was thinking, 'No, don't go.'"

"We walked and ran. They had a fence round the farm. We leaned on this gate, and was getting our breath when a big dog came bounding off the verandah, and rushed up barking."

"We was too frightened to move, let alone open the gate and go in," Thelma said. "Banner told us to let it bark, someone will prob'ly come. Sure enough, this man came out and whistled to his dog, walking quick-way."

"He slowed down when he saw us," Banner went on. "When he come closer I noticed he looked at us strange-way, made me feel no good, I knew my face was going funny, you know, real guilty. I wanted to take off there and then. These other four never noticed anything, you should have seen them, standing there smiling at him. They had no koondang."

"Yeah, we never notice him looking that way at us, we just thinking about having a feed."

"When I seen you fullas smiling at him, I felt like punching you and knocking you right out. Choo, talk about shame. That man asked us, 'Hello girls, what can I do for you, where did you spring from and where are you off to?'

"Brave one here," Banner pointed to Bella, "she telling that man, no shame about it, how we got lost looking for wood, with the mob back home in Boolaring, not very far from here, and talking flash-way to that wadjala asking him could we have a drink of water and something to eat?"

Bella took it up, "He never asked us where we come from, unna you girls? He just said we look tired bunch and we must be hungry. 'Come on up to the house, I'll get the wife to put something together for you, for breakfast,' that's what he told us."

Banner butted in, "I never said anything to that man, while we were walking up to the house. I didn't want to go inside, I kept tugging on your skirt, Bella, to slow you four down, not to follow that man. But no, all they was thinking about was food," she turned to us, "walking up to the house behind that man real greedy-way, so I never said nothing. Me, I knew what was going to happen."

"Why, how did you know?"

"Because you know that white family, they come to our church every Sunday. They come in that old black shiny car." We all sat there on the bed with screwed up faces racking our brains.

"They got all them mans in one family and that little fat boy. You fullas always laugh at him when he goes past you up to the altar for Holy Communion. You know, he wears them baggy trousers."

We all started giggling. "I bet you must have been scared, Banner." We knew that mob all right.

"Scared? That's not the word. I was so frightened I felt like bolting. All I could see was Father Albertus' face and Sister Ursula rounding up on me. I never ate their breakfast." Here

Banner pointed to Zelda, Bella, Thelma and Nicky, "These hungry ones, when that woman came in with bacon and eggs for us, she couldn't put the plates down fast enough. These big shots ate flat out."

Nicky burst out, "After stale semolina or bread and milk every morning, we couldn't help it, hey Banner, unna Zelda, sis and Thelma? When we saw bacon and eggs that finished us, we couldn't let that tucker go cold. We even picked the crumbs off the plate where that kind woman put our toast."

"No koondang, these fullas had. Never mind. When that woman left us alone in her dining room, I said to them, 'You know what? I wonder if yous will eat dry bread that quickly?' They looked at me silly-way. 'What you mean, Banner?' I was trying to tell them all along that these white fullas came to the mission church. 'Bet you any money that farmer is ringing up now. Father Albertus be on his way to pick us up and take us back. That's why he never asked us where we came from. He knows us all from Sunday Mass.'

"You should have seen the looks on their faces," she told us. "They nearly gave up right there."

"I never thought those white people were like that," Zelda protested. "They was so kind, she gave us all that tucker and she even let us have a shower."

"That's how white people are, and that's what you get for being greedy," Banner told her. "Anyway, not long after that, in walks Father Albertus and Brother Edward. These fullas started crying straight away. Father told us, 'Get up. Go und vait in zer ute. I vill deal viz you vhen ve get back.'

"With the help of Brother Edward we were in the back of the ute in no time. He made us shame. He grabbed our dresses by the back and lifted us from the bottom and chucked us in like rabbits. We felt shame because that farmer man was standing there. The way Brother heaved us in, our dresses come right over our shoulders and we went flying into that ute. Thelma banged her head and screamed out loud. Brother Edward just gave her a rabbit chop and told her to keep quiet."

Thelma butted in, "It hurt, feel this lump here?" She bent her head towards us. We all felt the bump, which was still quite big. Banner finished the story of our runaways.

"Soon as the ute turned up the old mission road, we started crying. I felt sick again, and I wished we had never stopped at that farm."

Especially to zer Ringleaders

The week of punishment for everyone in the dormitory was over. For a couple more days nothing happened. We were all in school when the bell started ringing at eleven o'clock, too early for the midday meal. Wondering what was going on, we heard Sr Petra telling us to put all our books away and to follow her over to the kitchen, so we knew there would be no more lessons that morning.

This particular day seemed all so strange. Looking out through the louvres, we never saw any cars outside, so it couldn't be visitors. Banner, Lilly, Sally, Bella and Nicky glanced at one another, shrugging their shoulders and flicking their hands from side to side, behind the nuns' backs, as we filed out one by one in a line. That was our signal when we were unsure of anything.

As we marched, Sr Petra shouted orders that we were to go into the kitchen and stand in a group over to the left side of the big table. That's where the most room was. The other nuns and brothers were already there. Sr Ursula took over from Sr Petra and told us to stand in a ring around the open space in the kitchen. With puzzled looks we took our places. We didn't know what was going on.

Looking very stern Fr Albertus strode through the door. The stomping of his army boots shook the floorboards of the old kitchen, as he swung his walking stick into the air, with every furious stride he made, until he was standing out the front, facing us. He looked real wild, his face red as a beetroot, and his false teeth were clicking louder than usual, his white hair was sticking straight up. We had never seen him like this before. He bellowed, "Bring me a chair!"

We watched Br Edward collect the iron chair from near the sink. Sr Gertrude the cook used to sit on it to supervise us when we used to pod the broad beans. The normally bustling kitchen was quiet, the nuns and brothers and all the pots and pans were still.

As Br Edward carried the chair out to Fr Albertus, there was no expression on his face, it was hard as a rock but this was Br Edward's normal self, for he hardly ever smiled at us. Nevertheless, to me it seemed he looked quite eager to fetch the chair.

Fr Albertus took it from Brother's hands and placed it sideways in front of himself. He said nothing to Br Edward, who walked back to his place. We were all pressed up tight, side by side, with no idea what was going to happen. We held onto one another's hands. I glanced at Banner but she looked just as confused as the rest of us. An eerie feeling cast a shadow over us, a sense of unease at the gloomy atmosphere of the room.

"Banner, get out here!" Fr Albertus made us jump. Banner hesitated and looked at us girls like she'd seen a ghost, her face went pale and I felt her hand go limp as she let go of mine.

"Vill you hurry up Banner? Get out here or I'll drag you out."

We could see Banner tremble as she put her head down and walked step by step, slowly out there. She stood awkwardly in front of the chair, not sure of what she had to do. Her fingers twitching nervously, she fumbled at the hem of her skirt, her face full of mystification.

"Bend over zer chair!" Fr Albertus' powerful voice sent vibrating echoes over our heads and around the kitchen.

"Let zhis be a lesson to all of you!"

The blue veins stood out on his face as he wrenched Banner's dress up, to her shoulders. I watched it fall loosely over her limp frame, as she lay across the chair. We gasped out loud. I turned my head away and glanced quickly at the nuns, because Banner's bloomers were in full view for everyone to see. I saw their red faces flinch.

Again Fr Albertus roared out.

"Zhis iss vat's going to happen to any of you girls who run avay again, especially to zer ring leaders!"

Then Fr Albertus' walking stick was coming down hard and vicious over Banner's slumped body. We could feel the wind of the stick with every strike he dealt. Nicky and Bella covered their faces. I noticed the tears trickling between their fingers. With my head down I could feel a lump loom in my throat as I listened to Banner's whimpers. Fr Albertus continued thrashing her. My eyes started stinging and I let the tears flow silently, watching as they splatted down on the wooden floorboards.

There was one loud crack and the hitting stopped. I looked up with misted eyes and saw Fr Albertus chuck what was left of his stick down on the floor with the piece that had broken off it. Without a word he stormed out the room, the same way he came in.

Br Edward then walked over, with what I fancied was a smirk on his face, and picked up the broken parts of the walking stick. He chucked them in the wood box, which was near the door of the kitchen, as he and the other brothers walked out. In the mission if you were punished by a priest it was a bad thing, especially the Rector, who was the boss. Us girls just stood there sniffling and wiping our eyes.

Sr Ursula went over to Banner, pulled her dress down and told her sharply to get up, go to the bathroom and clean herself up. I noticed a faint catch in Sr Ursula's voice as she spoke, while Banner struggled to get up off the chair. Sister sort of half helped her to her feet. Banner's eyes were swollen and red, but I noticed she was not crying like the rest of us, who were still finding it hard to wipe the tears from our eyes.

Sister told us to get cleaned up too and stop our sniffling and crying. If we weren't in line when the bell rang we'd miss dinner. We watched Banner's bent and limping frame go out the door and went after her in silence. Sr Ursula did not follow us.

When we reached the bathroom we found Banner slumped on the cold cement floor. As we gathered around her she burst out crying. "Mummy, Mummy, I want my Mummy!" She rolled around in pain. We all fell down beside her and cried with her.

Zelda and Poppy rushed to get our towels off their hooks. I got up and helped soak the towels in water while Lilly, Sally, Jackie and the rest sat with her. Banner stopped crying as we sponged her welts with the wet towels. Every now and then she'd let out a whimper, as we'd accidentally press too hard.

"Why didn't you scream and cry loud when Father was hitting you?" Poppy asked.

"I didn't want to let them know I was in pain, I didn't want them to see me crying."

Nicky and Bella cut in, "We feel sorry and real bad, it should of been us that got belted not you."

"Don't worry, we are all one family here," Banner started to cry again and so did the rest of us. Looking at Banner lying there with blue and red marks over her body, I got a different feeling about Fr Albertus. Why did he change from a loving, kind, thoughtful person, always smiling and giving us lollies and marbles, to a cruel vicious person?

Can You See zer Bullet?

A month after Banner's belting she had to help Fr Albertus in the garden, with some of our group. Before we started our job, Father called us all over to him, near the old fig tree. We all stood in a bunch, in front of him, as he leaned on his rake.

"Girls, I am going to burn off today. Vhat I vould like you to do iss rake up all zer leaves und rubbish, und Banner you can organise these younger girls, make sure zhey do zer job properly."

I noticed when Father was talking directly to Banner, his face seemed to go a deeper red, his eyes seemed to go over the top of her head, straight to us.

"Also girls if you find any unspent bullets lying around, see like zhis one, bring zhem to me." With the left hand he reached into his top pocket, took out a live bullet and held it up between his index finger and thumb. We all leaned a little closer to get a proper look, except Banner, who didn't move. She didn't even look up at Father.

"Banner, can you see zer bullet?" She just flinched and nodded her head. Father explained that the crows were damaging his apples, therefore he had been shooting quite a lot of them. With my eyes fixed on Father I got a sudden urge to secure my ging which was tucked safely in the back of my bloomers. Unknown to Father, we scored more hits on the apples than the crows. Father put the bullet back in his shirt pocket, along with a few that he had already found when raking up. Just before leaving, he told us to pile the sticks, leaves and dead grass outside the garden fence.

"Banner, start zer girls off in zheir job please. Vhen you have zer heap ready, send one of zer girls up to fetch me. I'll be in my shed, preparing zer hoses for zer burn-off." I wondered if Banner had heard. She was still not looking at him.

Banner told us younger ones to look for the bullets, while

she and Lilly raked up. Sure enough, we found some and went to give the bullets to Banner. Still very quiet in her speech and manner, she told us to dig a hole near the fig tree and put them in there, and to continue carting away all the rubbish.

"Don't forget to pile it high." There wasn't much talk and I felt strange because usually when we worked together we messed around, laughing and joking. This particular day Banner just didn't seem to be herself.

Our job took ages and we were all hot and sweaty by the finish. Banner told Lilly to get the bullets out of the hole, take them to Father and tell him that everything was ready for the burning. Father must have joined about three hoses together to reach the pile of rubbish. The nearest water tap seemed miles away.

Sweat was pouring out of Father's face, his shirt was drenched and clung to his back, and we could see Father's sweat sores through it. All the time we were growing up in the mission, he suffered with sores. He always wore a long-sleeved shirt. He had them on his hands too, but they weren't so bad there, compared to his back.

Father took a piece of rag out of his trouser pocket, to clean his glasses. With his face screwed up and eyes squinting, he told Lilly to help with the burning off, and Banner, Jackie and me to start cleaning up around the grapevines, near his work shed. Banner was already walking away. Jackie and I had to run to catch her. We leaned on her shoulders.

"Banner, what's up? How come you walked away? Father Albertus was still talking. I thought he was going to jar you up." Usually if you walked away from any nun or priest in the mission while they were still talking, you would cop a hit.

"I couldn't care less. I got nothing against you girls but I can't be myself any more when I see Father Albertus. I can't seem to face him." We walked in silence. Banner's belting flashed through my mind and I got cold shivers.

When we reached the shed, Banner wanted a drink, so we walked to the tap and held our cupped hands under it. From there we could see clouds of smoke billowing into the sky.

We wandered over to the grapevines but Banner said that she didn't feel like working. We didn't mind that and sat down with her in a shady spot. Then we heard a big explosion. Lilly's cry for help came from the direction of the fire.

We all jumped up and Banner was the first to bolt, with Jackie and I flat out behind her. When we got there, Lilly was crying hysterically, pointing towards the fire, stuttering something about Father. Banner rushed over, leaving Lilly to Jackie and me. Amidst trying to quieten Lilly, I heard Banner sing out to the rest of the girls.

"Run down to the mission. Get the Sisters. Get help!"

Shaking, I ran over to the fence. Through the smoke I could see Banner kneeling beside Father who was lying on his back, near the edge of the fire. Banner was holding up his right hand, which she had covered with her apron. I could see blood pouring and a terrible fear whelmed up inside me. I stood motionless, hanging onto the fence. Next minute I felt this stick land right across my hand, which brought me back to my senses. Banner was roaring.

"Come here, Sprattie, quickly!"

I got there but my legs went to jelly. I plumped down beside her.

"Sprattie, pull yourself together. Sorry I had to chuck that stick at you, but you wouldn't stop screaming."

"Was I screaming?" I kept my eyes glued to her, because I was frightened to look at Father, thinking he was dead. I always feared the worst when someone was hurt.

"I wish Sister and Brother would hurry up. Sprattie, did

those other girls go down to the mission for help?"

"Yes."

"Now come close to me and hold Father's hand up."

"I can't."

"Hold it up!"

"I feel terrible, look at the blood. What happened?"

"Sh– sh– " She put her finger up to her mouth. Father started groaning, and I said a silent prayer that he would be all right. Jackie and Lilly finally arrived on the scene with the rest of the girls and whoever else they had met on the way. A couple of nuns knelt down beside us, their faces shocked.

"Girls, vat happened? Aagh..." Then Brother arrived.

"Albert, Albert, can you hear me? It's Edward." Fr Albertus groaned and opened his eyes. A pang of relief surged through me. Brother asked Father if he could stand up and walk a few steps. He had driven the ute around the boundary of the garden fence. We all supported Father onto his feet and us girls milled around him as he walked slowly to the ute. Br Edward went over to the fire to collect Father's glasses and hat and came back with bits of the frame, all in pieces. He couldn't find the hat.

Lilly explained to Brother that a log had been sticking out of the fire. She saw Father bend over to push the log closer to the flame. We noticed how Brother's face was sickly white as he waited to hear.

"Go on, Lilly."

"I saw something fall out of his pocket, into the fire. Then quick he grabbed a stick and used it to poke that thing and try to drag it out of the fire. Then I heard the bang and I saw Father on the ground ..." Lilly burst into tears again.

Br Edward ran over to the ute. As we followed he turned and told us to walk back to the mission. Brother started the ute up. We were still pressing against the door. He told Sister he was rushing Father to hospital.

"It iss too late to save his zhumb and finger."

I went all wobbly in the legs when I heard that. Banner hung on to me because I nearly went out to it. I had seen the finger and thumb and pushed them into the fire with a stick.

"You all right, Sprattie?"

"It must have been a bullet that fell out of his pocket and went off." I felt like vomiting. The other girls looked pale too.

"He must be in a lot of pain." Banner put her arm around me. "I know the feeling, I've been through it." We all stood with our arms around one another, watching the dust of the ute disappear. Then we headed for the mission.

While Father was away Sr Ursula ran things at the mission. When he came back from hospital he wore a black sock over his right hand. We often saw him resting on an old bench in the yard. Father had made the bench in the early days, in a circle around the big redgum tree.

Brother Coming!

As we grew older, the sisters used to get us girls up very early in the morning to go and help the brothers in the dairy. Winter season was the worst because Wandering Mission in winter looked like it was snowing. It was picturesque to have everything white with frost but the water turned to ice, and in those days we never had shoes. So we caught chilblains and frost bites on our feet, as we had to walk about two miles away from the mission to round the cows up from the bush.

Br Edward used to come with us to help. He was tall and pleasant but he could get very impatient and give us rabbit chops on the neck if things didn't go his way. These cold mornings did nothing to settle his boisterous ways. Sally, Florry, Poppy, myself and Banner were the main ones for dairy duties.

It was huge, this place. There was a shed where the brothers stored bags of mash to feed the pigs, yards where the cattle used to wait, the bull yard where bulls were locked in and the calf-pen and chook yards, all in a big radius. When we reached the milking shed, Br Edward would bail the cows in for us; Poppy and I went to the feed shed and made sure all cows had a full bin while being milked.

I had two favourites. Magpie was called that because she had the black and white colours of a magpie. Golden Star was light brown on most of her body but a big golden patch on her back looked like a star. They were both timid and seemed to understand us. Whenever we were out playing in the fields and called their names they came wandering up to us.

After filling the cow bins with hay and mash, Poppy and I helped the other girls in the actual milking shed itself. There were about twenty cows. The little baby calves we used to lock in a separate yard till we'd finished milking their mothers. Br Edward would come into the shed to make sure we were at work while Br Victor lit a copper to warm the water for us and the cows. Then he'd boil it to wash the separating machine later.

Before we started milking, each girl had to wash her own cow's udder and teats. We sat on these little stools and buried our heads on one side of the cow's belly, balancing the pail between our knees. We let our knees take a firm grip, and with both hands would squeeze their teats with a striking motion, as the milk splashed from side to side. When the pails were full, we'd carry them in to Br Victor in the Separating Room. The machine he used looked like a flying saucer with two spouts, one for the milk and one lower down for the cream.

Inside the separating machine were these disks hooked onto wire mesh running all the way round inside. On the outside Brother put real fine netting material to keep all the grime and dust out. He turned a big handle to work the machine, which made a low buzzing noise. He would never let us turn the handle or use the machine. Our job in the Separating Room was cleaning up and bringing in the milk. I used to love fresh cream and when Brother ducked out to the milking shed I couldn't help but scoop a handful of cream into my mouth.

How scared we were of the cows when we first started work in the dairy! I think they sensed it too. One of my jobs was to shovel up the cows' droppings and Banner would stir up the cow she was milking if she knew I was coming close down the line, behind the hooves. I hated working with Banner because she would get us into trouble just for the fun of it. Many times I copped a rabbit chop from Br Edward over kicked buckets of milk.

I nearly ended up lame once when Banner stirred up this

cow while I was waiting with my shovel and broom at the back of it. She hit it with a stick and the cow caught me unawares. I cried out in agony and Br Edward came running with the girls.

"Vhat iss zer matter viz you, girl?" He pulled on the sleeve of my dress. I couldn't stand. Sally helped me up. My foot was swollen and bleeding from a gash by this time and they helped me into the old Willys jeep to be driven to the Dispensary. Banner was sitting behind the railing outside stifling her giggles.

Around this time more girls and boys came to the mission. Two years before, during 1958, the first six boys had arrived. Now my group of girls felt our home wasn't ours any more. Br Edward put a bar across the middle of Our Lady's Truck, so the boys sat up one end and the girls up the other when we went for our picnics or visits to town. Although the boys were segregated from us at meals, church and play, and even at school until the last few years, we still had some fun together, especially when boys came to the dairy.

Sometimes they had to help us in the milking shed. There were not enough girls for the work, especially if someone was ill, because the nuns had so many other jobs for us. So even though we never really had close contact while working with the boys, in the dairy we found ourselves near enough to muck around and have a laugh. That was when Br Edward wasn't looking.

Brother walked around from place to place, making sure that all was in order and that the boys stayed on the jobs they were given, as far apart from us girls as possible.

The boys were like us girls, always messing around and looking for mischief. Mallee and Gerry were lanky brothers. Their knee-length grey flannelette shorts, held up by a pair of braces, suited their lean, tall frames and knock knees. They both had big brown eyes, pointy noses and thin lips. All the boys had the same haircut. The brothers or Fr Albertus cut their hair, short back and sides but a bit left long at the front, which didn't do much for their ears, as they used to stick out like flying saucers.

Mallee and Gerry were also very clumsy, forever dropping things or not looking where they were going and stumbling over objects in front of them. They were high-spirited and either one or the other would be getting a belting for knocking over a pail of milk or dropping eggs when collecting them. This used to send us girls off giggling, getting us in a teasing mood for the rest of the day.

Jimmy was the first of the six boys to arrive and his bigger brother Jason came soon after. Listless and dreamy, they were brothers of Lynn and Lola, and the youngest of the boys, with big black eyes, broad noses and shapely lips. Their dumpy fat bottoms made their knee-length shorts look like balloons.

When we were in trouble for messing around, even though they never joined in with us, Jimmy and Jason would end up getting a flogging too, for being in our company. They were too slow to move out of the way. We'd get the warning from the look-out kid, "Brother coming!" and be off like shots. They'd be sitting there in a daze.

Teddy and Brian were more or less like Mallee and Gerry, thin, scrawny and rough. Their baggy shorts looked as if they were hanging off a bean pole. And those haircuts. Not that we could say much — the nuns used to place a plastic bowl on our heads and cut around it. In those days us girls either felt winyarn or solid, so it didn't matter to us, but the boys, ridiculous wasn't the word.

Br Edward started the old tractor, loaded the trailer up with hay and headed out to the feeding paddocks, which were a couple of miles from the dairy. Soon as he was out of sight, Banner put her two fingers in her mouth and let out a sharp whistle, which I am sure echoed down the valley all the way to the mission.

Boys and girls came from everywhere around the dairy. When we reached Banner she was perched on the rail of this yard where the baby calves were penned. It was just outside the Separating Room, and opposite the main milking shed. Therefore we could see the road that led out to the feeding paddocks and Br Edward.

Once we'd all taken our seats on the rails around the yard, Banner and the older boys Mallee and Gerry ran into the yard, caught a young calf and rode it. Sally, Poppy and Thelma ran in for a turn and the rest of us were laughing.

"Solid, choo, keep riding them, Poppy you're solid!"

"Choo Banner, you deadly." Banner tried to stand up on their backs and ride, with her dress tucked into her bloomers. Then she fell flat on her back and we killed ourselves laughing. The boys liked showing off in front of us girls by doing different tricks, like trying handstands on the calves' backs. Half the time they'd be lying on the ground groaning. We'd run and pick them up and struggle to put them back on the calf again, ignoring their aches and complaints.

When we'd had enough of that, we ran to the haystack, climbed the ladder and swung from the rafters down onto the hay. We all loved playing in the haystack, it was good fun. This time, we made Jimmy and Jason stay on the ground to keep an eye out for Brother. They were too slow in warning us, so we belted them. That was after we'd been belted ourselves.

Then there were a lot of changes. Boys took over the dairy altogether, girls were put in the laundry, kitchen and sewing room. No more dairy duties for us girls. Bad enough that the nuns used to lock us in the dark rooms for our punishment; let alone having to sit and help mend the clothes with four walls around us.

Real Solid and Neat

Another change which we couldn't quite take to grips, was the coming of teachers. A lot of the girls and boys from the earlier times didn't worry about it so much, because they knew about teachers, they'd already been to schools. They were taken from those schools and brought to the mission by their parents, or with the help of dedicated Christians and white Native Welfare Supervisors, on the grounds that the kids were better off growing up the good Christian way, and our people's way of life was no good.

Most of the newcomers had also been to schools, where they were taught by whitemen teachers. So it did not come as a shock to them so much as to us, when we were told in the dining room one day by Fr Albertus that Sister Petra would no longer be teaching us. She was going to take up a post in Perth.

Our new teacher would be arriving the next day, a Saturday. That would give Fr Albertus enough time to show him around the mission on the weekend and he could meet us kids on the Monday. We were to call him Mr Pitts. Father hoped we would be on our best behaviour. A two-storey building would be added to the fathers' dining room, to be used as classrooms.

"Next veek anozzer teacher iss arriving from Pers. His name iss Mr Foley and he vill be taking zer smaller grades until zer new buildings are ready. For zer time being he vill teach in zer girls' recreation shed." This was a corrugated iron shack not far from the rubbish tip, used by the girls in winter for play and to relax in.

That night we sat on Banner's bed.

"Hey, you fullas, I wonder what this man teacher gunna be like?" said a puzzled Thelma. We'd never had a man to teach us before, apart from the priests giving religious instruction.

"I hope he is kind and don't hit us like them sisters." First Sally, then Ruby spoke up. She had not long arrived in the mission. "Where I come from is a little country town in the wheatbelt and me and my cousins went to a school where we had a man teacher."

"What was he like?" we all eagerly asked. Ruby sort of screwed her nose up in the air, shrugged her shoulders and in a deep-drawn audible breath told us how she and her cousins were always in trouble with that teacher.

"We never liked him, because he let them white kids call us black boongs and niggers."

"What does that mean?" Being so innocent and vague, I didn't know what she was talking about. Ruby looked at us.

"Choo, Sprattie and you other fullas, don't you know what nigger and boong mean?"

"Nah." We smiled at her in a real simple way.

"Well all you fullas are niggers and boongs."

"Hey, how come?"

"Well, because ..." Ruby fiddled with the corner of the sheet, which was hanging over the side of the bed, "... that's a sling-off word used by them white kids at school for us people who are dark."

"Choo." We looked at one another, we'd never heard of that before.

"Now you girls know, for later on."

It sort of never really sunk in, as I listened to Ruby carry on about her teacher not listening to her or her cousins, how they used to belt the white kids up for calling them those names, and their teacher always took the white kids' side. Banner scoffed.

"What? I hope our new schoolteacher not gunna be like your one, Ruby."

"Nah, I don't think so. He can't be like that, because we are all dark here."

"Hey Banner, just make up, if this new one hit you, what will you do?"

"Thelma, I'll wait till he turns his back, then I'll run up behind and hit him over the head with a piece of wood and knock him out, so he can't move, and then I'll knock piss out of him. He'll be blacker than you, Thelma."

"Choo." We all killed ourselves laughing.

Saturday morning came, with excitement and whispers in the air. The dining room was like a beehive. Us kids didn't take long in gulping down our bread, milk and sugar, which was all mixed together in a huge pot made up in the kitchen. Whenever Sr Gertrude was on duty she would stress to us that back home in the little German village where she grew up, her parents fed her on bread and milk every morning and it was good for us too, as we'd all grow up to be healthy and strong girls.

Sometimes she would soak our bread with buttermilk, which we loathed, especially for that first meal in the morning. I would rather have faced a bowl of sauerkraut. Whatever we were having for breakfast, be it semolina or bread and milk, it would be washed down with a plastic cup of white sugary tea. That was also made in a big pot. Sister would pour out the tea, making sure none of us got more than the others. Sometimes one of the kids would be slow at eating or drinking, and we would think nothing of helping ourselves to their last drop.

After the meal, we all stood beside our places, which was a regular thing after and before our meals. We'd recite with Sr Ursula our thank you prayers to God for the meal.

On this day, before we could start, Sister raised herself up and down on the heels of her black shiny laced-up shoes.

"You all know zhat today iss a special day, because our new teacher vill be arriving. Fazher will deal viz zer boys. I vant all girls to carry on viz zheir shobs as usual. You all know your Saturday duties. Vhen zer new teacher arrives, I don't vant any of you girls coming out of zer building oontz running up to zer car oontz staring. If I see any girls hanging around zer car vhen zer new teacher arrives, which I think he vill be arriving after dinner, zhen zhere vill be trobble!"

While she spoke, the two fore-fingers of her right hand tapped the left palm, and her darting eyes pierced straight through us. My stomach squirmed when I saw her in one of these moods. She had a habit of pin-pointing a person out in front of everyone, and I'd get real shame, whether it was me or not. Her loud voice echoed through the dining room.

"You ringleaders know who I mean when I say you vill be strictly punished if you disobey my orders. Glenysen Sprattsen, Banner, Zhelma, Lynn, Sally, Florry and Poppy, do I make myself clear?"

"Yes, Sister." I could tell the others were sniggering at us. We murmured our thank you prayers, "We give Thee thanks, Almighty God, for these and all the other gifts which of Thy bounty we have received, through Christ Our Lord Amen."

Everybody went to their various jobs. Banner, Thelma, Lynn, Sally, Florry, Poppy and myself cleaned the dormitory. This was a spring cleaning day, which meant all of us had double jobs. We had to change all the sheets on all the beds, and take the dirty washing to the laundry. We took turns carrying it away in big wicker baskets. Then we washed the entire walls. Then we waxed and polished the floor.

Our group didn't mind working in the dormitory because we mucked around quite a lot. When it came to polishing the floor, we would take turns pulling one another around on old jumpers, to put a shine on the floorboards. That was after having rubbed the wax into them on our hands and knees.

Besides, we could see clearly out the windows if any visitors turned up.

All morning we kept peeping out during the work. In one way we were glad to have a different teacher, not that we could say anything against Sr Petra, but it would be a change from getting our ears pinched and being pulled from our seats by our cheeks.

The midday meal came and our teacher had still not appeared. Us girls were back in the dormitory, straightening out things, getting ready for Sister's inspection. Jessie, who was a new arrival, came banging on the door.

"Quick, you girls, open up, there's a car coming, quick!"

"It must be him," yelled Banner, running to open the door. She slid the bolt back. We used to lock the door from the inside to keep out other girls and to give us time to stop any mucking around if Sr Ursula came to the door to check on us. We would find some excuse to tell her why we had locked the door.

"Get in here," Banner grabbed the excited kid by the hand and flung her inside. We nearly fell over one another getting out of Jessie's way. Not waiting for her to catch her breath or say any more, we pushed one of the double-decker beds up to the window. Our spick and span bed-making looked like a bomb had hit it, as we pulled and struggled with one another for a good possie to look out the window.

Every time a visitor came to the mission we would get really excited, and if we weren't jumping all over their car, we'd be peeping out the windows of a building like animals in a cage. The light and dark blue two-tone Holden pulled up outside the fathers' and brothers' monastery. We could see everything from where we were perched on our bed.

"Look at those boys all standing round the car." It was Banner's wild tone. "That's not fair, unna you girls? Them boys think they great."

"I reckon they are spoilt, they get petted up all the time by them nuns and priests." Sally dug Banner in the side.

"They got no shame! That man can't get out, they baulking him. Besides, they are in our way, we can't see what our teacher look like." Banner had the best position at the window and stared out at Teddy and Jimmy standing right at the car door. I could see Fr Albertus coming out of the monastery. Thelma gasped.

"Baalay, look out now! He gunna make them boys scatter."

We all fell silent, pressed against one another, putting up with the discomfort. Father walked over to the car, gesturing and calling to the boys to move aside. The car door opened.

Our teacher got out, and we noticed that he was tall, well-built, strong and good-looking. He extended his right hand to Fr Albertus, who gave it a good shake, but with his left hand. Father's right hand was tucked away inside the black sock, in the pocket of his brown khaki trousers.

Father ushered up the boys, pointing them out as he introduced them. Again the teacher held his hand out. The boys hung their heads in shame, scraping the dirt with their feet as they put their own hands up weak-way, for the new teacher to shake. Us girls killed ourselves laughing at their antics.

"Choo, choo. Them boys look winyarn. They got no koondang."

The boot of the car was up and the teacher placed his cases on the ground. Father organised the bigger boys to carry them away to the monastery, where he had prepared a vacant room. Then the two men walked across to the buildings with the rest of the boys crowding around them.

"Baalay, quick, Sister coming!" Thelma sang out, so we jumped off the bed and two of us pushed it back quickly, while the others made the covers on it straight again. Sister walked in to a nice clean and shiny dormitory with everything shipshape.

The weekend passed. Although we never officially met the teacher until the Monday, we did have a good look at him in church on Sunday, when he strode up to receive holy communion. Us girls stared at him cruel. He was bald in the middle part of his head but around the sides his blond hair was thick and wavy. He had clear crystal blue eyes and stood expressionless in his pew. From what I saw he looked hard and stern, but then in those days I thought almost everybody looked like that.

Religion was different in those days of the Latin mass, there were no smiling faces. It was a sin to laugh and talk in church, everyone was so serious and reverent. I thought, he might be different when we get to school. After mass we were back in the dormitory changing out of our tunics into Sunday best dress.

"What you reckon about him?" Thelma sang out, "Were you watching him in church when he went up for communion?"

We didn't get a chance to answer. The working girl we called Silkie overheard us talking. She came rushing in and sat down on the bed. We all froze because we thought we were going to cop it.

"Listen here, you kids! I don't care what you think or say about him ..." She had this real sheepish grin all over her face as she grasped one of the girls round the waist in a cheeky way and sat down on the bed. "... from what I saw of him, I reckon he looked real solid and neat."

Then she burst out giggling and bent down and gave me a hug, as I was sitting there on the floor in front of her! She stood and picked up the hem of her dress and twisted it round her body so that when she twirled herself round and let go of the dress, it all spun out, and we saw everything from her legs up to her bloomers. She went chuckling out the door.

Our minds were so innocent, we never said anything, we

carried on getting ourselves dressed for breakfast. It seemed real strange to see Silkie acting this way. Most of the time she walked around strict and stern like the nuns. Very rarely on occasions she'd do things out of the ordinary, like sneaking off for swims with us in the dam. All these changes going on around the mission left me with a frightening confused state of mind.

Koondang

Monday finally came. The school bell rang as usual and before we took our place in the school line-up, we got our last lecture from Sr Ursula on our behaviour for the day.

"Sister Petra vill be still viz you for anozzer week, to show zer new teacher, so he can get used to zer school. She vill report to me, if zer new teacher needs to discipline any of you."

In Catechism, for an hour before actual school lessons started, we were very nervous and confused, trying to concentrate on Father Gustave, a new priest, as he preached to us about God. When that was over we stood at our desks and said thank you to God. In the mission we not only prayed before and after meals, we prayed before and after school lessons. Fr Gustave stood in front of the class.

"Now girls und boys ve vill say a special prayer to thank God for sending us our new teacher, so zhat Sister Petra has finally found a vay to furzher her studies, oontz zer new teacher can teach you children his knowledge oontz skills."

After prayers he walked to the door, opened it up and Sr Petra and the new teacher were there outside. The three of them walked into the classroom while we were all still standing by our desks. "Good morning Sister Petra!" we answered back in a singsong to Sr Petra's greeting.

"Now say good morning to your new teacher." Mr Pitts stood there, tall and strong, his white cotton shirt tucked neatly into long grey pants. He had a dark maroon tie and pointy brown shoes, and his hands hung down in front, one across the other. There was a grin on his red face and his blue eyes sparkled.

"Good morning." The voice was deep and loud. "I gather by now you all know my name." We all sort of laughed as he went on, "I come from a place called Benderton. I don't suppose any of you come from there, or have even heard of it?" We all kept quiet. "Well, I am known as a headmaster. Do you all know what that means?"

"Nah." We smiled our winyarn way. He looked at us strangely then.

"Well, we won't go into that yet. I will tell you as the weeks go by. First of all I'd like to know your names."

Fr Gustave excused himself and left the room. Sr Petra stayed. For the remainder of the day we went through our work, with Mr Pitts grading us to see how far we were advanced. He singled out the younger ones like myself, to be taught by Mr Foley, who would arrive later.

The week went by. Every night in the dormitory, after lights out, we talked about Mr Pitts. I was glad to be going with Florry to another class at least for a year. The rest of our old group, Banner, Poppy, Thelma, Lynn and Sally were all in Mr Pitts' classroom, but in different grades.

When the weekend came a couple of us were already in punishment for misbehaving and found ourselves doing extra jobs on the Saturday, like making butter. That was a thing I hated, for it meant standing at the butter box a couple of hours, turning the handle instead of playing out in the paddocks with the other girls.

The idea was to pour a four-gallon can of cream into the box and then keep churning until it turned into butter, while my mates peeled buckets and buckets of potatoes and skinned onions. We would end up stiff and sore from standing or sitting so long in one place.

On Sunday, instead of our usual walk in the afternoon, all the boys and girls had to assemble down at the convent to farewell Sr Petra. We had afternoon tea with her under the shade of a big redgum tree, where the nuns used to have their meetings. We had helped them to make flower beds and put garden chairs there.

Sr Petra's last words to us were that she hoped we'd concentrate and listen to our new teachers and do the right thing. She would pray that one day we might end up in one of the Perth schools, and if so to come and see her, as she would miss us all and would be thinking of us.

"It vill make me very proud if my Vandering girls can make it to Perth grades. At least zhen my teaching vasn't in vain."

Another Monday came, and all the younger ones lined up over by the old girls' recreation shack, to be marched in by yet another new teacher. He had arrived over the weekend, in a small green panel van, with his wife and baby daughter. They were to live in a red brick cottage, specially built up near the boys' dormitory.

Mr Foley was also tall, had black hair and was a jumpy sort of person. When he was angry he held his left shoulder with his right hand and moved it in an abrupt manner, as if he was in shock. That used to frighten us. I remember how Mallee frequently copped it. Mr Foley was forever picking on him and we thought he hated our mate Mallee.

Once the whole classroom smelt really bad and Mr Foley walked around with his shoulder twitching, up and down the aisles of our desks. He shouted at the top of his voice, demanding to know if we had all washed properly, or if one of the younger kids hadn't made it to the lavatory? He snapped the louvres open and swung the wooden door wide for fresh air. We all just sat in our chairs like frightened mice as he stormed over to the windows that faced the dump.

"That smell is horrible. If at any time anyone needs to go to the toilet, you are to let me know straight away."

After school, Florry and myself had the job of cleaning the classroom. We tried to brighten up the old shack by going over to the bush nearby and picking some Blue Leschenaultia and

Yellow Hibbertia sprays. We thought the scent of the flowers might drown the horrible smell.

We collected some old jars from the dump, washed them out and put them round the room with the flowers in them, placing one on the teacher's desk. Florry went to set another on the window ledge nearby, where there was already a pot plant. It was some sort of creeper that Mr Foley had brought from the city and was it growing! The stems bent over and hung down all round the sides of the pot with thick leafy foliage.

"Florry, be careful, don't touch the pot plant, you might knock it off the ledge and then we'll both be finished."

So Florry put her vase on top of the book cupboard instead. We stood back.

"Everything look right. Our teacher shouldn't get wild now, unna Florry?"

"Too bad about that old dump."

Out we went to play and thought nothing of it until the next morning. As we filed in we could all sense Mr Foley was upset. The putrid scent hit us straight away.

"Before you girls and boys sit down, I want you all to take a good look at this stick here. See this?"

We looked in our frightened way, as he held out a flat piece of board as long as his arm. It was really thick.

"Right, the name we are going to call this is Waddy."

He banged the waddy hard down on a pile of books on his table and we all jumped. Suddenly a boy interrupted the speech with a startled cry. We thought one of the other kids had trodden on his toes. We all looked around.

"I didn't mean to do it, Mr Foley!"

It was Mallee. Foley stormed over to him with the waddy still in his hand, got him by the back of his shirt and dragged him to the front. All of us watched terrified as this man shook Mallee like a rabbit and bellowed at him to tell everything. Mallee was choked up, blurting out between his sobs that he had pee'd in the teacher's pot plant.

"When did you do that?"

"When you went over to Father's dining room for morning tea, the other day." Mallee's voice was quivering. "We were having a game of fly and I didn't want to miss out. It was too far to go to the toilet and there was no girls around. I come back in the class and couldn't find an empty bucket so I saw your pot plant and I thought I'd water it for you."

For the first time Mr Foley brought the waddy down hard across someone's bottom. Mallee screamed.

"That is a horrible thing to do! Don't you know what a toilet is? Next time it happens you'll be locked up with the pigs. Get that pot plant and go and chuck it out on the rubbish heap and then get yourself back here quick smart." The teacher's face was red and his veins sticking out blue. We stood watching as Mallee limped over to the plant with his head down, rubbing his eyes.

"In the meantime, this —" Mr Foley slammed his waddy down again, "— is a lesson for all you others. Now hurry up and sit down at your desks." The lesson continued with Mallee in a corner by himself, and there he stayed all through the day.

The following night we were huddled on Banner's bed, discussing the teachers.

"I got told off just because I asked Banner if she had a spare nib pen," said Thelma. When she dipped her own pen in the ink pot she had banged too hard and broken the nib. "Mr Pitts separated me from all the other girls and you only thought it was funny, unna Banner?" Banner laughed.

"Sorry sis but I couldn't help it, when he sat you on the floor in front of the class. I just wanted to stir Mr Pitts up to see how wild he gets." Banner turned to us all. "Thank God for when

I become a working girl. I can't wait for the year to pass, can you?" Lynn, Thelma and all the others who were in the class with her agreed. Then Banner turned to me.

"How is your teacher?"

"I don't know, he's only been here a week but I hate him. He's cruel, unna Florry?" All the other girls wanted to know what happened. I didn't want to say. We had all been taught that it was very bad to talk about someone, especially nuns, priests and brothers. It would be a sin to tell about our teacher and if anyone was caught they would be punished.

"Florry, you tell them."

"Carn, Florry," everyone said.

"Okay, but promise not to pimp on me, promise true God?"

"Look, true God," Banner and Thelma and the rest solemnly blessed themselves and spat into their pyjama sleeves.

"Our teacher, he nearly killed Mallee. You know how our room smells? We thought it was the rubbish dump because we used to it, but our teacher, that stink was making him sick." Banner started to giggle.

"Banner don't laugh, our teacher he made us shame, unna Sprattie? I didn't know where to look when he asked all us girls and boys if we never made it to the toilet. He thought one of us goona'd ourself, choo, talk about shame! You notice how all them boys were looking at us girls, choo, big shame."

By this time Banner was killing herself laughing. All the other girls were serious. We were all used to Banner and let her go, smothering her laughter in a pillow. Florry told how Mallee had burst out crying in the classroom.

"What happen then, what happen?" One of the little girls who wasn't in school at all had asked this. Florry grabbed her pyjamas from the back of her neck and wrenched her up.

"Ouch, God that hurt, Florry."

"Well that's how Mr Foley lifted Mallee. Fairly shaking him. You fullas should have been there and seen how he dragged him out. He owned up and told Mr Foley what he did to the teacher's pot plant that he brought from Perth. Winyarn! Talk about koondang. Next minute old kid just got flogged with that thick stick. He made us all sorry, unna Sprattie?" Soon as Banner heard that she killed herself laughing all over again.

"Choo Banner, keep quiet, one of those other girls might tell Sister on us, then we'll all cop it." We couldn't stop her.

"I can't help it, can't you see the funny side, good job Mallee done that to your teacher, that's just what he needed."

I think all of us girls saw the funny side then. Suddenly we burst out laughing. I mean it wasn't like me to be laughing when I felt like crying. It used to upset me to see one of my mates hit, and Mallee was with us from earlier times. Even when we were out in the playing fields and one of us was hurt, I used to be the loudest one. Everyone would think it was me that was hurt. I felt like crying for the fact that Mallee got belted but couldn't help laughing like Banner.

A New One to Us

The following Friday we all had to go over to the bigger classroom, to join the older kids, so Mr Foley led us over and jammed our class in the front of the room. We all stood quietly, with Mr Foley's eyes glaring down on us.

Before Mr Pitts delivered his speech he bent forward from the waist in a peculiar way, with his hands behind his back, like an emu stalking out something shiny on the ground. Then with a sudden lifting motion of his head and in a deep voice he bellowed out, "Good morning, boys and girls!" We all answered back with a singsong, "Good morning, Mr Pitts."

I happened to glance at Banner. I could see she was trying hard not to laugh because he looked so funny. Thelma dug me in the back, making it very hard for me too. Mr Pitts walked with long slow steps, his arms folded behind his back. Up and down, up and down in front of the classroom, where we were all standing.

"Every second Friday, we are going to have what they call an Assembly. The school I have come from held Assemblies, so we shall do the same. Assembly will be every second Friday."

Us kids had never heard of the word, it was a new one to us. We stood looking at him like stunned mullet. He had stopped dead in his tracks, with his left hand resting on his hip.

"Do you all know the meaning of the word Assembly?"

"Nah," we all chorused in our giggling, smiling way. The smiles soon disappeared. Mr Pitts' right hand furiously stroked back the long strands of his blond hair, that normally lay over the front balding part of his head. He rushed over to his desk and picked up a long, springy rod. His blue eyes were intense as he cut the air with the whistling cane.

"Now, I will ask you all again, and you are to answer me in a proper manner of speech!" He thrashed the cane down past the right side of his body. "This is one thing that I am going to change in your school, and I am sure Mr Foley will be doing the same. We are going to teach you all to speak proper English, none of this 'nah' business when you are being spoken to or asked a question. You are to say 'Yes sir! No sir!'

"And another thing. What does this 'choo' mean? Last week when I held up one of my paintings, during our art lesson, all I could see were these grinning silly faces all saying, 'Choo, choo!' You don't know how stupid you all look and sound.

"Another word I do not want mentioned in either Mr Foley's class or mine is the word 'unna'. What sort of language is that? Unna! A sort of language that has to be stopped. I will get very annoyed if it is said in my presence. And if I do hear it, maybe a few reminders from my friend here will refresh your memory." The cane swished as he held it out and turned himself around so that all of us had a clear view. "Do I make myself clear?"

"Yes sir." We all spoke together.

"Now, as I was explaining to you about our Assembly, we will be gathering outside the classroom every fortnight for discussion on different topics. For your information, Assembly means to gather together and talk about things. Discussion will be followed by singing. We shall sing songs about Australia. And now I think we will just run through some of the songs that you already know. Could one of you boys come out to the board and write the names of the songs you have been taught by Sr Petra?"

Teddy stood up and strolled down the aisle to the front. Mr Foley ushered his class to the back of the room to make way for Teddy and Mr Pitts to use the board. Us girls thought Teddy was a showoff. He was in Grade 7 and thought he knew everything. He was so sure of himself as he slouched on down the aisle, with his hands in the pockets of his grey knee-length shorts, thinking he was great because all of the girls were looking at him. There was a smirk on his bony face as he stood by Mr Pitts in front of the blackboard.

Then Mr Pitts grabbed him by the front of his collar.

"You walk down the aisle properly, with your hands out of your pockets, and don't put on the smarty-pants act with me, is that clear?" Teddy's bold character turned to shame as Mr Pitts jarred him up. We could see his face going funny.

"Yes, s-sir." Mr Pitts let go of him. Teddy stumbled back and clung to the teacher's table to stop himself from falling over altogether.

"Now get yourself over to this board and write the songs down. There's plenty of chalk, get on with it."

Mr Pitts stormed over to the corner and picked up a peculiar shaped object. It was wide at one end, skinny at the other and with both sides curved in at the middle, with a case-handle to it. All eyes turned away from Teddy, who was shaking like a leaf as he tried to write a song up on the board. We were curious to know what Mr Pitts had inside this strange box, which he opened up. It was lined inside with purple velvet and clipped to the underside of the lid were two long curved brown sticks which seemed to have elastic stretched along them, going from one end to the other.

Then he lifted from the box a brown object, hollow and made of wood, with thin wires all in a row, running up to some knobs at one end. Mr Pitts lifted this object right up to near his ear and pressed his cheek into it. Then he unclipped one of the long sticks and rubbed the elastic part of it up and down on the hollow wooden object, making the queerest noises. We had never seen or heard anything like that in our lives and all burst out laughing, especially at the expressions on Mr Pitts' face.

We were so busy laughing we didn't notice he had stopped making the noises and was standing there furious. A complete silence spread over the room. Mr Foley was holding his shoulder and shrugging it. Mr Pitts spoke almost in a whisper.

"What is so funny?" No-one dared to answer him.

"I think you are the most rude, arrogant lot of children I have ever met."

He Might Come in Here

At the end of the following week, our teacher said he was taking us mushroom picking, because his friends were coming from Perth and they loved mushrooms. He would only take a few of us, three boys and three girls. I loved gathering mushrooms, but I dreaded that he would choose me.

He picked Penny, one of the new girls to our school. Then he picked Gina and then me. Three boys were to come with us, Jimmy, Brian and Billy. Mr Foley told us all to go over to the big redgum tree. He was driving home to get changed. We were to be waiting there when he returned. We weren't to worry about buckets, he would bring the buckets.

I liked Penny. She was tall and lanky, a highly strung girl who often told me how she missed her baby brother. He was still back home in a country town, south somewhere. She had asked her mother if she could bring him with her next year, after the holidays. Her mother had said it was bad enough letting the priest talk them into sending Penny away, let alone her brother. She had said, "Home is where Mum and Dad are."

Gina was another girl who had only recently arrived at Wandering. She was plump, always laughing and joking, that's why I got on with her. Both Penny and Gina shared my feelings about Mr Foley. They came running behind me and pulled at the sleeve of my jumper.

"Sprattie, where you going? We supposed to meet sir and them boys at the gumtree remember?" The rest of the kids had gone out to the fields to play but I was walking slowly down to the bathroom.

"I feel sick, I'm not going."

"Choo, come on Sprattie, you always loved picking mushrooms. He gunna get wild if we not there."

"Don't worry about me, you two go ahead and if he ask where I am, tell him I'm too sick to go." Next I heard their footsteps following me into the bathroom. They got on both sides of me.

"We don't want to go either! Let them silly boys go, never mind if we get into trouble." So they said but they were frightened.

"He might come in here and find us."

"Don't be silly. I been here longer than you. No man's allowed in the girls' bathroom, not even the priests or brothers come in here." We all sat back on the bench and laughed about the boys, thinking they must be in Mr Foley's green panelvan by now, speeding off to the paddocks by the dam, where the mushrooms grew.

"Can you fullas picture them sitting in sir's pretty car, winyarn-way."

"I don't fancy sitting all squashed up with the boys in the back of that van. Our Lady's Truck is the best, hey? No other cars can beat it."

Our conversation was interrupted by the banging open of the wooden door. Mr Foley pounced on us, dug his hand into our necks and sent each one of us flying out of the bathroom.

"Are you girls deaf? Didn't you hear my orders? When I say or tell you to do something, you had better do it!" Too shocked to say anything, we walked over to his car, with a shove in the back from him every now and again to hurry us along. The boys were already in the panel van, sitting bunched against one another to make room for us.

We climbed in slowly, shameful-way, careful not to show anything personal of ourselves. Mr Foley stood there pulling his shoulder. He made sure that we were in the car, huddled in a bunch, before he slammed the door and stormed around to the driver's side. He started the car and took off, catching us off guard. We suddenly ended up on the boys' laps. Deeply shamed, we quickly got back to our normal position and clung to one another as the old car sped along a dusty gravel track.

There was no division between the front seat and the back of the van, so we could see ahead. Every now and again I noticed Mr Foley glancing through the rear vision mirror at us. It made me feel no good inside and I concentrated on the scenery of trees and hills flashing past. I changed my position to sit upright with my legs out straight, facing the boys, who also had their legs stretched out. I tried to keep my feet from touching theirs.

The boys thought it was a great joke to see us in this uncomfortable position. They could sense we were unhappy, which gave them all the more reason to poke fun by pulling tongue at us when Mr Foley wasn't looking, or pressing with their feet when we swung around a corner.

All the time they looked at us putting a brave face on, and knew full well that if we were anywhere else other than sitting in the teacher's car going flat out, we would have dropped them right on the spot for what they were doing.

We kept driving till we came to a clearing with paddocks on both sides of the track. Mr Foley leaned back suddenly and shouted, "Which is the best spot?"

"Wandering Brook, sir, not far from here."

The boys all spoke at once, blocking our view as they knelt forward, crowding over the back of Mr Foley's seat to give him directions. We sat listening to their jabbering.

"If you just go a little further sir, you'll come to a big gate. You can drive down to the big dam and park there. We find lots of mushrooms there, unna you girls?" They all looked behind at us and we nodded our heads. The car came to a standstill and we were glad to get out and stretch our legs. Mr Foley gave us the buckets and told us to go get mushrooms.

"You boys go in that direction. I'll come with you girls." Our hearts sank. We just put our heads down and walked off slowly, all the way making sure we didn't get out of sight from the boys. Mr Foley kept following us around. Every now and again he would find a few mushrooms himself and come over to drop them in our buckets, making sure he either brushed one of us on the arm or came really close. We were relieved when we had a bucket full.

At the back of the van, waiting for Mr Foley to open up, Gina bent down to pick up her bucket of mushrooms.

"Hang on, Gina, I'll give you a hand with that." The teacher closed his hand over the top of Gina's as she grabbed the bucket handle. I could sense Gina's alarm.

We were into our early teens and still naive about many things. The boys used to watch the teachers' attitude towards some girls, and watch us girls too, sly-way, sniggering and carrying on silly-way behind our backs, saying how the teacher must be mardong for us, and we were jirruping for him. On the way back the boys sat smirking and grinning. Yet for once in my life I never minded the boys teasing us, I could put up with that better than getting those sickly looks from Foley.

There were no smirks back at the mission that evening, as we walked past their tables to get our tea. I was relieved but I also knew that the reason they didn't smirk at us was because the nuns were there. Over the weekend Jimmy, Billy and Brian were teasing us in the paddock about the mushrooming and Mr Foley.

"Choo Penny, he love you, shame!" And all the boys started laughing and singing out to us, "Shame you girls, you must be solid."

We had separate playing grounds, joined by a fence.

Whenever the boys would see the girls in the paddock, they'd automatically run to the fence and start cheeking us, and this younger girl Trina shouted back, telling them to shut their mouths.

"Billy Rice, Brian Leathe and Jimmy Neal, you fullas tight on your own. We don't want that ugly-looking thing. Gurn, you come over here, we'll make yous jump, unna, all you other girls?"

By this time a few more girls stopped playing games and came over to join with us and ask what was going on. Trina told them how the boys were teasing us about Mr Foley dragging us out of the bathroom. We walked away from the fence because we saw Sr Ursula coming towards us from the convent with one of the big girls, who was Trina's cousin. Trina broke away from our group and ran to her cousin. So it was that Sr Ursula got wind that we'd disobeyed Mr Foley and hid in the bathroom, instead of waiting at the gumtree.

Over the weekend we heard nothing more about it. We were getting dressed for school on the Monday morning. Gina and Penny came over while Banner was combing my hair.

"Hey Banner, what if us girls was getting dressed like this and our teacher walked in?"

"Oh, I wouldn't know what I would do but I do know one thing, you wouldn't catch me in that classroom after, I don't care what happens, they can flog me all they like, it wouldn't matter, I am used to it, what would you two do?"

Gina and Penny said that they would tell their mothers and fathers when they went home at the end of the year.

"What would your mother and father do?"

"They'll come here and knock them teachers flying, they not frightened," Gina pouted her lips, full of confidence. "Mum got a brother and I seen him having a fight with three big rough wadjalas down the street outside the pub, because they was gunna mob dad's cousin."

Suddenly a voice made us jump.

"Glenysen Sprattsen, Gina and Penny, stand where you are. You other girls can go and line up for school."

We three stood in fear as Sister went over and waited for the last girl to go out. She shut the door of the old tin bathroom and turned to us, her face scarlet.

"You girls tell me vhat happen in zer bazhroom zer ozzer day. One of zer big girls told me zhis morning vhat's going on." My heart sank, for I was expecting to be hit. Words came stumbling out of my mouth.

"Sorry, Sister, I never listened to Mr Foley. He told us we had to go mushroom picking with him. I didn't feel like going because I wanted to play a game of rounders with Banner and them other girls." I thought to myself, any excuse is better than none at a crucial time like this.

"Zhen vhat happened, girls?" Sister wasn't even interested in my excuse. Still trembling, I went on to explain how I got the girls to come toilet with me and how we sat down on the bench. I looked over to Gina and Penny for support.

"Oontz vhy did you sit down on zer bench, girls, knowing full vell zhat Mr Foley vas vaiting for you?"

"Penny had a splinter in her foot and it was hurting her, so me and Gina was getting it out for her."

"Lift up your foot, Penny. I vant to see zhis splinter."

Taken off guard, a bewildered Penny turned her back towards Sister and lifted her left leg from the knee, with her left hand holding her foot back, so the sole was turned up. I stood in front of her to give support and she clung to my shoulder to keep her balance. I could feel the fingers of her right hand digging in as she glared at me. This was how we turned the soles of our feet up for inspection of stone bruises, cuts and cracks to our heels, which we often had because we did not wear shoes.

Knowing full well the condition of Penny's foot, I ignored her eyes and bowed my head to join Sister in looking for the splinter that wasn't there. Sister's two fingers kept prodding hard into Gina's foot.

"I can't see zhat zhere iss anyzhing wrong viz your foot. You komm zhis afternoon to zer Dispensary oontz ve can bazhe zer foot in zer tob, zhen ve vill know if your splinter iss still zhere, or not!"

Penny gladly put her foot down and stood up straight, while Sister walked to the basin, turned on the water and rinsed her hands. Then she reached into the long sleeve of her habit and pulled out a white hanky which she always had tucked away there, to wipe her dripping hands. The look on her face was serious and her voice stern.

"Vere any of you girls really sick? Vhy did you behave in zhis manner towards your teacher? Glenysen Sprattsen, you haf been here zer longest, you know zhat zhere iss a punishment for disobedience oontz you are setting a bad example for zer new girls zhat come here." She put her hand up under my chin to lift my bowed head up. Her piercing eyes burned down on me.

"Tell me zhis, girl, did Mr Foley come in zer bathroom to get you?"

I got a sudden bout of nerves.

"Yes, Sister." I couldn't stop blinking.

"Did he see anyzhing of you girls, vere you getting change?" Feeling real shame, I said softly, "No Sister." She released my chin and my head dropped down again. Quick as the wind, her voice came soft and kind.

"Ach, girls, if you vere feeling sick, vhy didn't you tell zer teacher, zhat vould haf solved all zer problems."

"I kept telling the teacher all morning my belly was aching but he wouldn't listen to me."

"Girls, zhis iss enough talking. You may go to school, and

not a word to anyone vhat ve haf been discussing."

Only too glad to escape, especially without a hit, we bolted out of the bathroom shack like wild horses. The next weeks in the classroom, we three girls found ourselves doing extra duties. Mr Foley seemed to have us in mind whenever a job came up.

What Is the Matter with You Lot?

The year with Mr Foley was up for Florry and me. Some of the girls and boys went back home. They left the mission altogether. Banner and Thelma had left school to work with the nuns, helping out in the kitchen. Never mind, we still had Poppy and Lynn when we joined Mr Pitts' class.

By this time Mr Pitts was in his brand new classroom, a second storey on top of the little girls' dormitory. I was glad in one way that I was in Mr Pitts' class because my sister Sally was in the next grade and around me most of the time.

Mr Pitts started the year off by putting us in mixed groups, girls with boys, something we had to come to terms with. Before that we had never sat close to boys, we were kept segregated in the classroom. Now Jimmy, Billy, Florry and I had to sit together. When we were used to sitting next to one another, the girls and boys mucked around something wicked. One of our group was always dragged out of the desk and made to sit on the floor in front of the class.

I noticed the teacher's attitude was more furious on a Monday. Sometimes I wondered what could be upsetting him so much? I would try double hard at my work, but seeing him like that I became nervous and made a whole lot of mistakes. For the rest of the day our bodies used to suffer from Mr Pitts' cane.

Fridays were different. One Friday morning he told us that after doing our sums we were all to follow him into the dining room. We just carried on doing those sums, we couldn't think about anything else. As usual he stalked around the room checking up on us.

So after sums we all followed in a line behind Mr Pitts, who was carrying that object of his in a case. He had told us it was a violin. We entered the dining room through the back door and filed to our usual places, along the neat long tables.

"All you boys and girls, I want you to shift the tables and chairs over to one side. Hurry up, and make it quick."

He laid his case on one of the tables, removed the violin and fiddled around with it, while us girls helped carry over the benches to make space. Mr Pitts told us to sit on the floor in front of him, while he sat on a table.

"Right, I suppose you must be wondering what's going on." He ran his fingers through his loose blond hair and flicked it over the bald patch. "Every second Friday you all know that we have Assembly. Well, now on the other Friday, we will have dancing. You are going to learn a few dances. These we call square dances."

Mr Pitts babbled on about how he would like us to dance at Assembly, and also when the school inspector came later in the year. We were to sing songs and do dances, just to show the inspector that we could do something.

Florry kept digging me in the ribs as Mr Pitts made himself comfortable sitting on the table, with his legs dangling. I thought to myself, if the nuns saw him sitting on the table like that! Would he get into trouble? When we cleaned the dining room, us girls would take a break and perch ourselves on the tables like that, with legs up and feet resting on the benches. If we were caught we'd get a flogging from the nuns. A table wasn't meant to be sat on, it was a place where people ate their food, and it wasn't ladylike for us to sit like a man, they said.

Mr Pitts' gruff voice broke my thoughts up.

"Very quietly now, I want you to pick your partners for the barn dance, which we are going to learn."

He turned his back on us, to get his violin ready, and we all excitedly ran for our best mates. I grabbed Florry's hand.

Other girls grabbed their mates and the boys did the same. Teddy and Jimmy were partners as they came over and stood beside us giggling and messing around us.

Mr Pitts turned around, as we stood there smiling winyarn-way, holding hands with our mates. His face abruptly turned red and he slammed down his bow. We heard it hit the table and thought he had broken it.

"I said take your partners! For a dance! And that means boys with girls, like this – " He tore around the room, grabbing girls and distributing them. He shoved me by my shoulder over to Teddy and put our hands together. He continued on like that, putting girls with boys, till everyone had a partner. Choo, I never felt so ashamed in all my life.

This was the first time that we ever learnt to dance and hold hands with a boy. Talk about koondang. Mr Pitts played some quick music on the violin, and we just all stood there staring at him, not knowing what to do. I looked over at Thelma, standing there holding hands with Jimmy. Her face looked really stiff and embarrassed. I gave her a grin. Mr Pitts stopped playing.

"What is the matter with you lot? I have never met such a dumbstruck mob in all my life." He put the violin down. "Right, you boys, go to that side, and you girls come to this side. Make enough room, so you can skip down the middle."

We all formed a line, girls on one side, boys on the other, facing our partners.

"Now, when I start playing the violin, I want you, in pairs, to take your partner and skip down the middle, to the end of the line, boys to their side, girls to theirs. Clap your hands to the beat of the music. We will go through this routine a number of times until you have all had a turn, and until you all get used to it!

"Then on the following Friday we will learn another step, because I can see it's going to take me a long time to teach you lot anything that will stick in your thick brains."

He turned suddenly and walked over to my sister Sally.

"Now we will go on to one other step. Before I start playing, this is what I want you to do."

He grabbed her by the hand.

"Choo! Choo! Waadow!" We all shouted. I could see Sally feeling shame as he walked her to the top of the line.

"Right, you get your partner by the hand like this. Sally, we are going to skip down the middle. All you other lot start clapping."

He looked so funny skipping that Sally was too shame, she just ran beside him and disappeared back to her spot. We all burst out laughing, thinking it was a great joke. Mr Pitts walked to the front and turned on us.

"Haven't I told you before about this silly attitude you all have? That word 'choo, choo!' That expression is driving me mad." He raised his hands in the air and his big blue eyes poked out. He looked funny. Some of us kids couldn't control our laughter and still had our hands covering our mouths.

"I am warning you now, I am not going to warn you again. If I hear stupid sniggering and going on, I won't hesitate to thrash the living daylights out of you. Glenyse Spratt, Florry Jacks, you can wipe those silly grins off your faces, or I'll wipe them for you."

We clammed up, and he lifted himself on to the table in a sitting position, then swung himself around and stood on the table top, in his shoes and all.

"Right, I can see you all from here, so look out." He lifted the violin to his shoulder and was about to play when a voice sang out. "Ohhh waa!" We all looked around to see where it came from. Poppy was standing there with her hands over her mouth. By the look of things I think she didn't mean to sing out.

"Right, I want the person who sang out to come forward."

All our eyes were on Poppy as she went to the table with her head down and stood in front of Mr Pitts. Still standing on the table, he glared down at her.

"Poppy Turner, what's this 'ohhh waa' business?"

Poppy rubbed her foot on the floor.

"Put your head up when you are being spoken to."

She lifted her long face up and her black eyes shone out.

"You are not allowed to stand on the tables, Sister always hit us."

"Well, is that right, Poppy Turner? So she should hit you, you are an arrogant mob, cheeky and very rude. And another thing, Poppy Turner, what gives you the right to speak to a person in authority such as me? Do you know what authority means, Poppy Turner? Answer me!" We could all see sir was steaming, his face was red. "Nah," Poppy said in her shy way.

"Well let me get this through your thick skull. I am your teacher, and nobody, nobody, tells me what to do. If I want to stand on the table, I'll stand on the table, and I don't want a snotty-nosed brat telling me otherwise!"

With that outburst, he jumped down from the table and took the waddy in his hand. Everywhere he went he took that waddy with him. He grabbed Poppy by the shoulder, swung her around and gave her a few cuts across her legs.

"Any more outbursts from you, Poppy Turner, and look out. That goes for the lot of you." He climbed back on the table and dancing lessons continued in a state of gloom for the rest of the morning.

At night in the dormitory when the lights went out, we were all on Poppy's bed yarning about our teacher, which seemed to be the usual topic of late. Banner wanted to make herself more comfortable and leaned down hard on Poppy.

"Ow, Banner you hurting me." As Poppy pushed her off, Banner started laughing.

"Don't laugh, her legs are sore. She got belted from Mr Pitts today," I told her. Banner grabbed Poppy.

"Sorry sister, I didn't know about that. I didn't mean to laugh at you, you all right now?" Poppy pulled her legs over the other side of the bed so nobody would hurt her again.

"Never mind," Banner said, "me and you will be together next year because you'll be a working girl, and you won't have to worry about him any more."

Poppy

Mr Pitts explained to us one morning that we would all be receiving the *Young Readers Digest*. He said that the stories we had read in the *Happy Venture* books were for the smaller kids and this new book was more suitable. I didn't mind the blue-covered *Readers Digests*. I found stories in them like *Robin Hood, Treasure Island* and *Tom Sawyer*, really exciting.

So I was all for it when we gathered around Mr Pitts in a group, while he sat on the chair and listened to us read aloud. Sometimes I used to play dumb and make out that I never heard him telling me to stop, when it was someone else's turn.

Poppy had a terrible problem, stuttering, especially when it came to reading lessons. Everyone was standing so close to her and staring all the time, waiting for her to make a mistake, it came time for punishment. Watching Poppy struggle nervously over her words was no joke. I glanced at Mr Pitts' face. He was agitated and I started to feel uneasy for Poppy. Sure enough, Mr Pitts interrupted her.

"Come closer, stand in front of me here."

He was seated with his legs crossed and his pointy brown left shoe raised close to her.

"Right, Poppy Turner, start reading again out loud and clear, so I can understand you, and stop that stupid jabbering."

Very frightened, Poppy continued on with *Treasure Island*. Her voice went shaky. Suddenly Mr Pitts lifted his foot. The full force of it sent Poppy and a couple of girls flying, as they caught her falling. She lay limp on the ground in front of us.

Our mob learned to deal with our punishment no matter how serious it might be. Poppy, stunned and shocked, got to her feet holding her stomach.

"And you had better start practising your reading more, otherwise you can expect worse to come!"

I bent down to pick up Poppy's book, which had fallen to the floor, so it was my turn to be roared at.

"Glenyse, you'd better put that book down where you got it from. Poppy Turner can pick her own book up. Or do you want the same punishment?"

I dropped the book down that quick, like it was hot toffee. He told us all to go back to our seats and continue the reading quietly. I heard Poppy grunt as she bent to collect her book. As I walked past her I let my khaki hanky fall to the floor. Back in my seat I put my head down and tried to concentrate on reading. I glanced across and Poppy was drying her eyes with my hanky.

The nuns made these hankies for us because Sister Helga, who was now in charge of the laundry, said she was sick and tired of the results of our using the seams of our jumpers or the hems of our dresses, to wipe our noses. So we were all given hankies to take to school, especially as Mr Pitts had also complained to the nuns that there were lanterns hanging from our noses, and they made him feel sick inside.

That night in the dormitory on Banner's bed, Poppy wasn't feeling too well but we were frightened to tell Sr Ursula. One of the big girls, Rina, heard us talking and came over from her bed to tell us all to get back under our covers and stop talking. Rina was a new girl to us, a working girl with Banner. She had only that one year in school at the mission and we didn't have much to do with her. She would give us things like a piece of apple or orange. Every now and then the working girls were allowed fruit with their dinner. The school kids had fruit only on special occasions, like a picnic.

Rina asked Poppy what was wrong. All us other girls remained silent, as Poppy hung her head. You couldn't complain about the teachers, that would mean punishment. Banner became impatient.

"Poppy, put your head up and tell Rina what's wrong with you. Go on, she not gunna pimp on you, unna Rina?"

"That's right, Poppy, I won't tell on you, I just want to know if I can help. You got a stone bruise or toothache, I'll go and get a tablet for you from Sister." Rina put her arm around Poppy's shoulder. Poppy stuttered.

"He boot me here, in my tummy, and I got a guts ache."

"Who hit you there, Poppy?"

"Mr Pitts booted her in the stomach, for nothing," Sally spoke in an even tone.

"Poppy, you not telling lies are you?" Rina looked Poppy right in the eye.

"Nah, Rina, why should I be lyin'? He hit me here, unna you fullas?"

"Yeah, Rina, she not lying, we all saw Mr Pitts just dropped her, and we all thought we was gunna get dropped too. That's why we never said nothing."

"Okay, you girls, I believe you," Rina said, "now all get to bed. Poppy, how you feel? If you still get pain, let me know and I'll go and get a tablet for you."

Before Rina went to bed herself, Poppy sang out, "Rina, you promise you won't tell Sister on me, unna?"

"I promise you," Rina called across the dormitory.

In the following weeks, leading up to the August holidays, there was a change. Sr Ursula took us for reading lessons in the dormitory at night. We didn't mind reading before we went to sleep, because we were allowed to stay up a bit longer.

When the Fights Started

A couple of months went by, our group just biding time in our world of uselessness. One Monday morning Mr Pitts added more confusion to our minds. He ordered all the fair kids to pick up their books and stand out the front of the class, while the darker-skinned ones had to help clear one side of the class for the fair ones.

He explained that he could do so much for the fair ones and besides, they were a lot brainier, and he had already wasted enough time on the darker ones. He had no great labour picking anyone from our group, because we were all dark. Jimmy, Billy, Florry and I walked slowly backwards and forwards, helping the others like Sally and Poppy to shift their books over to the desks on our side of the room.

Again I had this horrible feeling in my stomach as I glanced up at the line of fair kids standing there waiting with their piles of books in their hands. Megsy gave me a superior look. She was a newcomer. I never liked her ever since she landed at the mission.

I could see that Sally, Billy and Jimmy were wild. They made out they accidentally dropped a book, and slammed down a desk lid. Even when everyone was seated, fair to one side, dark to the other, we couldn't relax. My mates had sad, wondering looks. Mr Pitts was explaining.

"This will be the seating arrangement till the end of the year."

The fair ones were sitting up like proud peacocks. That's when the fights started amongst us kids outside the school. Us dark ones wouldn't talk to the fair ones, because they walked around the place thinking they were king pins and better. At breakfast one morning I overheard Megsy giving my sister cheek across the dining room table.

"Pass me the spoon, darkie."

Her skin was real fair, just about white. I shouted from my position.

"Gurn, who do you think you are? You just as black as us, unna Poppy and Florry?"

"You think you white but you just a poor black thing like us," they sang out in support. Megsy stuck her nose in the air.

"Shut your mouth, Glenyse Spratt, you got no right to talk to me about being black, look at you, you're not black, you're purple!"

"Ohhh waa, did you hear that? Get up and punch her, Sprattie. I wouldn't let no-one talk to me like that," Poppy whispered.

"Nah, I'll wait till after breakfast and get her in the bathroom, I'll make her piss."

"Gurn, don't tell us you're frighten of her, Sprattie?"

Megsy leaned over the table with her lip pouting.

"I'd like to see you try and hit me, because see this fist?" She held up her clenched fist, "It'll punch your black mouth in and knock you silly."

By this time, with all the arguing going on around us from the other kids, I saw red and slid down my chair, stretched out my leg and gave Megsy a hefty kick in the shins.

"Ouch, you bitch!" She jumped out, picked up her fork and threw it. Everybody ducked as the fork bounced off my head and I cowered in pain. She had made me bleed and all the time of my growing up in that home, I never felt so bitter and angry.

I picked up a china cup full of sugar off the table and with all my strength threw it at her. The cup split her forehead open, blood spurted out and Megsy started screaming. Now the whole dining room was up in arms. I just went mad. I jumped up and rushed around the table to hurt her more.

The full force of Sr Ursula's open hand made me see stars. She slapped my face to bring me to my senses and pulled me away from Megsy, who was crying hysterically.

"You go and vait in zer dormitory, Glenysen Sprattsen." She took Megsy by the hand and led her away to the Dispensary, leaving a couple of big girls to keep order in the dining room. My sister Sally and all my mates followed to the dormitory.

I sat down on a bed before I fell down. I felt really sick in my stomach. That was the first time I got into a real fight. At the mission any fight was a big thing amongst the kids. It was so bad in the eyes of the nuns that we could expect to be punished severely. They crowded around and Sally put her arm over my shoulders.

"Thanks, sis, for taking it up for me. Next time it's my turn. Don't worry about Megsy, she be quiet enough now, serve her right." Someone else squeezed my hand.

"Good job, Sprattie, you give it to her."

"Baalay, look out, Sister coming!" someone shouted. Everyone scattered except me. Whatever punishment was to be bestowed, I was ready for it. I started feeling sorry for Megsy and said a silent prayer, thinking I might have killed her.

"Glenysen Sprattsen, you know what you have done?" Ursie started with her lecture. I wasn't feeling too hot now. "You nearly killed Megsy. Vhatever came over you, girl? You vere never a violent person." Her softly spoken voice shocked me. Usually Sister's lectures were rough and boisterous, especially in a situation like this, after a fight.

"Megsy tells me you have been calling her names."

"I heard her calling my sister darkie," I said.

"Vhat iss zhis language, girl, darkie, vhat iss zhis meaning?"

"It means, Sister, that Megsy called Sally darkie and she said I was purple," I blurted out.

"Vell, ve have never have zhis kind of language here in zer

mission, vhat do you suppose Megsy meant by zhat?"

"She meant that we are black-skinned and she thinks she's white."

"Ah, I see!" Ursie exclaimed in surprise. "How did all zhis business start?"

"Well Mr Pitts told us in school that the fair ones were good and he can't do nothing for us black ones."

"Ach girl, zhis explains zer whole situation about zer unsteadiness of you children lately. All right, vait here vhile I call Megsy in." She was standing outside the door. Megsy walked in slowly with a big bandage around her head.

"Megsy Bruce, Glenysen Sprattsen has told me how zer fight started and I vant to hear from your own mouth vhat Mr Pitts told you all in zer classroom." When Megsy had finished, Sister made us both to kneel on the floor and say prayers asking God to forgive us for fighting. She made us promise not to fight again and gave us a parting lecture that we were all equal under God's care, nobody was different. Then we made up and said sorry.

"Zhis time girls, zhere iss no punishment for you, but don't let it happen again."

We were so relieved that tears spilled from our eyes and I could not stop crying. Especially when all my mates came to see what our punishment was. We sat on the seat in the bathroom just letting all the emotions out of our distraught bodies. They kept passing wet towels to us, to wipe our faces with. Pulling myself together, I managed to tell them what I had told Sister, and what she had said. Like us, they were very surprised that we weren't punished.

A month later Mr Pitts' behaviour was still the same towards us. The only change was that the fair ones were mingled in again. And we noticed that the nuns' attitude towards us was changing to kindness and understanding, which was a big shock to us girls.

Prayers

Sister would often interrupt prayers to tell us who we were to pray for, a sick girl or nun or priest, saying things like, 'Now girls, ve vill pray for Sr Erika's mother, back in Shermany, who iss very sick. Ve got vord from her family in zer home village zhat she iss not expected to live. Ve vill pray and ask God and his angels for her forgiveness.' We used to recite after Sister whatever prayer she was leading and think nothing of it, because we'd always be praying for somebody, be it in church or wherever.

One Monday night we were in the dormitory on our knees with Sr Ursula. When Sister stopped our praying, it was nothing unusual.

"Tonight ve are going to pray for a very special person, whom ve know oontz you know, zhat vhen he leaves us he vill be missed by all. He has done a vonderful shob here. He has made a big sacrifice in leaving his family in Shermany. Especially during the var years, vhere some of his family got killed."

With mystified looks on our faces we kept glancing at one another, wondering who she was talking about. Her bunch of keys rattled. Her hands were trembling. Sister was finding it hard to get her words out.

"He made his home in Australia, in dedication for you children oontz your people." We never understood what she meant by that, we were just hoping she'd hurry up and tell us who she was referring to. "By now, you all know zhat ve have a new priest coming. He vill be arriving in a week's time." Like a bullet it hit us.

"Oh no, Sister, not Father Albertus," we all cried out.

"Girls, girls," Sister raised her voice. "Ver-shoosh, ver-shoosh, quiet girls. You must understand, it iss zer vill of God, zhat zhis iss happening, Fazher Albertus knows zhat. His shob iss done. He came to prepare oontz make vay for zer new priest.

"Girls you must understand, trust in zer Lord, for he vorks in many vays. Oontz anozzer zhing girls, you must treat zer new priest like you vould have Fazher Albertus. Also before ve start our prayers for Fazher, somezhing else. Ve vill have a concert on Sunday evening in zer dining room for Fazher Albertus' going avay. Zer boys vill be joining zer girls in putting on zer concert."

When we heard this we were surprised, because we never did anything with the boys, we were usually strictly separated. Sister was trembling, trying to keep her feelings in. Her beads were rattling.

"All girls from Fazher Albertus' earlier days in the mission, Glenysen Sprattsen, Banner, Zelda, Sally oontz so on vill sing zer Kookaburra song, first learned when ve sisters arrived here. Now ve vill start prayers."

I found it really hard to recite the prayer after Sr Ursula. I was hurting real bad. The lump in my throat was getting tighter and tighter, I felt a burning sensation in my eyes as steamy hot tears welled out and splattered on the floorboards in front of me. Through misty eyes I glanced over at Banner and the other girls, who every now and again would bow down their heads and wipe their tears away with the bottom part of their pyjama jacket.

When prayers were over we said goodnight to Ursie and crawled into our wooden beds. I listened to her padlocking the door on the outside, then heard the footsteps going away.

I snuggled right down, pulled my grey army blanket over my head and burst out crying. I couldn't help it, knowing the person we loved so much was going away and we would never see him again. After a cry, I stuck my head out, bundled the pillow in my arms, stuck my thumb in my mouth and lay quietly looking back on it all.

"Sprattie are you awake?" Banner sang out. "Come here, we are on Florry's bed."

Every time we had yarns, it was on one another's beds, always on the bottom, because the top of our unstable double-decker beds might have given way with our weight. I jumped in beside Florry and Zelda with my pillow and started sucking my thumb again. Whenever I felt sad I sucked a thumb.

"Choo, Banner, we gunna miss him, unna you fullas? Never mind all the hidings he used to give us." Sally glanced at our gloomy faces. "Who gunna give us marbles and lollies now?" We cast our big sad eyes at May. At that time all our thoughts were on missing out on our marbles and lollies.

Banner broke the monotony by saying we could steal from the storeroom. Nothing surprised us any more about Banner. Even in the saddest moments we went through at the mission, Banner would be up to something.

"Choo, don't be like that, Banner."

"Nah, I feel real sad too, because after all said and done, he was the best. I forgave him for all the punishment he give me. At least he still kept being nice and giving me things after he hit me."

"Yeah, you remember what Ursie told us about God saying we got to love everybody even if they did wrong themselves. Otherwise the Devil will punish us."

"I wonder what the concert is gunna be like on Sunday?" Poppy piped up, going on about how she hated standing up in front of the boys singing, how it made her shame. We all agreed with her.

"They always make fun of us if we make mistakes, unna? They are real stare-bears and pretty kids." This meant they were all ugly. I stopped sucking my thumb and said, "What about that boy called Teddy, winking at any girl that walk past him, and digging us in the ribs when Mr Pitts not looking in the classroom. He think he solid, but he open, poor thing."

"Choo, you want to look out, girl, you're solid," Banner put her arm around me. "He must be jirruping for you."

"Gurn, who want that simple thing, I hate his guts, that's Thelma's boy." We all started laughing. The nuns never taught us about ourselves. Anything to do with boys used to make us feel real shame. We all just said, we're not gunna say anything to them or take notice of them, we'd think about our favourite priest, Fr Albertus.

The nuns never taught us about the facts of life. Being brought up strict Catholics, we were constantly being told that we weren't allowed to mix with boys, because it was filthy to be seen with a boy, talking and holding hands. We were never to say bum and had always worn long dresses so as not to show our knees and things.

Sometimes a few of the girls who had brothers used to talk to them and hug them, when they got the chance. I saw them getting flogged for that.

Just going back on one of my own experiences, this boy had a crush on me. Being so vague and innocent I didn't realise what was going on, although all the other girls must have sensed it, because of the way he carried on. I couldn't stand Billy Rice. He was fair in colour, and his light green hazel eyes had all the spark and mischief to match his lanky frame and brown spiky hair. Billy Rice liked playing pranks, especially when it came to being around girls.

When we had our Piece time, which was a break between lessons, the teachers would go for their cup of tea. Us kids lined up under the old redgum tree in the yard. Sr Gertrude and a big girl from the kitchen would give us our piece of bread and dripping or whatever it was to be that morning, sometimes jam or honey on occasions. We always called it Piece time.

Billy Rice would get one of his mates to chuck a tennis ball in our direction, where all us girls would be standing in a group. Then he'd run flat out, make-up way to gather the ball, and in his earnest process to retrieve the ball he'd pinch one of us on the backside. Now to us girls in those days that was really disgusting and horrible, because of the nuns' point of view on these matters.

Billy must have known I hated him, but he was the sort of boy who wouldn't take no for an answer. On those special occasions when we'd get an apple or orange with our meals, he would save his apple. When he saw the chance, he gave it to a mate to pass on to me, maybe in the playing fields or in the classroom. There I'd be at my desk, lifting up the lid and sneaking bites between lessons, pretending I was looking for something.

Although I had this real hatred for him, I wasn't going to knock an apple or orange back. We only were given fruit once in a blue moon. In the yard, all the girls who teased me over Billy Rice would come over. They'd look at me longingly, cadging for a bite.

"Gimmie some apple, sister girl, give us a bite."

"No, you fullas are not getting any apple from me."

"Choo, then you must love him, look how you're eating that apple, fairly taking big bites!"

Although I was boiled up inside me, I'd keep eating, then save the apple core, wrap it in my hanky, and wait till I'd see Billy Rice again. When he started his nonsense, giving me big droolly looks, I'd chuck the apple core and hit him right on the head. That didn't seem to stop him and his pranks.

Lining up for meals outside the dining room, he would set the whole thing up by standing in front of his mates. He'd get one of them to give him a shove and stumble into our girls' line, make out he was falling and grab me real tight around the waist. "Choo, choo, you must be solid," the kids shouted at me. I pulled his hair and broke his grip, giving him a shove back that sent him flying into his mates, and they'd all go down with him.

Rather than tell the nuns about Billy Rice, to save ourselves an embarrassing lecture, we used to live with it, keeping everything stored up inside us. One day in the dining room, a girl was teasing me, saying Billy was mardong for me and I was jirruping for him, which really got on my nerves. He flicked a piece of paper to his mate with a lacky band. His mate flicked it to me, but instead of reaching me, not that I really cared, it landed in front of the nun. I just kept drinking my tea slowly. Suddenly Sister told everyone to be quiet and pay attention.

"Who does zhis note belong to?" She read it out, "B.R. loves G.S., in a heart!"

Everybody clicked straight away and started shouting and yahooing, which made me real shame.

"Be quiet everybody. Glenysen Sprattsen oontz Billy Rice stand up."

Billy gave me a cheeky grin. I felt sick in my stomach and turned the other way. Everyone around thought it was a big joke.

"Billy Rice, you go straight avay to see Fazher. I vill explain to him on zhis nonsense. And you Glenysen Sprattsen, I vill see in zer dormitory."

The days that followed after my lecture turned me right off boys. I felt like strangling Billy Rice every time I saw him.

I Didn't Feel Like Singing

All week we were kept busy around the mission preparing for the concert, before which Father would celebrate his last mass. On Sunday afternoon the dining room was partitioned and hung with sheets to make a stage. This was decorated with fronds of Zamia palms cut in the bush. We plaited them and placed them in jam tins around the stage, amongst the gumtree branches which the brothers had chopped down and put into drums. The wildflowers we picked fresh from the bush. One of the bigger girls made a painting of the hills and drew some Kookaburras sitting in a tree. Finally everything was set and us girls went off to the dormitory to get ready for church.

The day being very special, we all had to dress up in what we called our Sunday best, a short-sleeved white blouse with a dark navy blue tunic worn over the top. It reached to just under the knees. Then we had white nylon ankle socks and brown leather sandals. We all had to wear a beret. The boys had white short-sleeved shirts, grey woollen knee-length shorts held up by braces, grey ankle socks and the brown leather sandals. What made us girls laugh were their way-out haircuts. The brothers used to shave most of their hair right off and only leave a little bit in front. We used to make fun of them cruel.

Us girls and boys were marched from our dormitories in procession and lined up outside the church. Boys in one line and girls in another. The neighbouring farmers started rolling up; they had got word that Father was leaving. Visitors came from far and wide. While we waited to let the farmers into the church, Banner gave me a dig in the ribs. A certain farmer was walking past us. We couldn't talk at the time, because all the nuns were standing behind us and if you were caught talking you'd be punished. So I kept it in my mind.

All the visitors were in their pews, kneeling down, the Angelus bell stopped ringing and us kids filed in, boys to their side, girls to theirs. We knelt down with all the nuns lined up at the back of us as usual, to make sure that we all said our prayers and did the right thing in accordance to God. Sr Erika, our choir mistress, started playing the first hymn softly on the organ at the back of the church.

At that time the service was in Latin, so we started singing in English and Latin while everybody waited for Father and his two altar boys, Teddy and Jimmy. They were getting ready in the sacristy, the little room off the top end of the church, which was also used to hear confessions. The two altar boys appeared in their full-length red robes and white starched embroidered long-sleeved blouses, looking serious. One carried the thurible, and the strong aroma of burning incense escaped through the holes on its side. The rich fragrance filled the whole church. The other boy carried the candle snuffer, and Fr Albertus followed behind. He wore his white alb, which looked like a smock. Over the top of that was a shiny green vestment with a bright yellow cross on it, in stitch work.

With his left hand he held a box-shaped article in the same green material of his vestment. This was the covering of the chalice, which the nuns had sewn at the corners with stems, like a yellow trellis. Every time I saw Father carrying the covered chalice it reminded me of a magician bearing his box of tricks. His right hand rested on top, in its black woollen sock.

As Father and the two boys made their way to the altar, we all stood up. Sr Erika broke the silence with the old organ, loud and clear. Everybody followed and again burst into song. I didn't feel like singing. Like most of them, this hymn had a melancholy tune to it.

"Thee oh Christ the Prince of ages ...
Thee the nation's glorious King ...

From our own dear land Australia
Drive the night of heresy ..."

I stood gazing as Father opened the tabernacle with his little key and the two boys sat on either side of the steps that led up to the altar. The music stopped playing, all was quiet. Everyone knelt down in their pews.

Father commenced the service and I noticed his voice didn't have the same effect he used when bellowing out prayers. In those days the priest celebrated mass facing the altar with his back to the congregation.

There were a few more songs before he stopped halfway through the mass and turned around to face the people. We all got up from our kneeling positions and sat on the benches to hear his last sermon.

"You all know by now zhat I am leaving you. God villing, I vill be going back to Shermany to my home village. I vant you children to be good und obey zer next priest who vill take charge of you after me."

His voice quivered, his face was red and every now and then he would nudge his glasses with their thick lenses. They seemed to hang loose on the bridge of his nose.

"Remember, children, I vill be zhinking of you no matter how far away I'll be. Zhis mission vill alvays be my home. I may not be in body here viz you but I vill be viz you in spirit. I love you, children, all very dearly, und don't forget I'll be taking viz me to Shermany many happy, fondest memories of Vandering."

Father rubbed his sock hand up over his weathered left hand in slow motion while he spoke, and I noticed how dusty flakes of dry skin floated to the floor in the rays of sunlight coming through the windows.

"Not to feel sad, because I know zhat viz all zer love und dedication ve brothers, nuns und priests haf given you children, zhat vhen you grow up und become big strong men und women, most of you vill make good vorkers on farms, like our visiting friends here."

Albertus put out his left hand in a gesture towards the farmers. There was punishment for looking back at people in church, but we couldn't help it, we glanced back at our visitors. They were standing up proudly with big grins across their faces, except for the farmer Banner had dug me in the ribs about, earlier on, when he walked past us to church. He looked grim. Banner glanced at me in bewilderment.

"Und zer girls vill make excellent cleaners I am sure, vhatever farm you vill vork at, girls. Remember all zhat ve haf taught you, und you vill make zer vhite people who you vork for very happy."

With good intentions running through my mind about becoming a domestic worker, I joined in a German song taught to us in our very early stages at the mission. The two altar boys were the first boys whom Fr Albertus had brought, when they were four years old. Now they were eight. They led the song, called *Lobe Den Herren*.

I was emotional, I used to cry when upset and this was a sadder time than any, as the words were bellowed all around me.

> "Lobe den Herren,
> den Maechtigen Koenig der Ehren,
> Lob'ihn Oseele vereint
> mit den himmilisolen choreren,
> Kommet Zuhauf,
> Psalter und Harfe, wacht auf,
> Lasset den, lobgesand horen ...
>
> Praise to the Lord
> the Almighty, the King of Creation,
> Oh my soul praise Him
> for He is my health and salvation

*All you who hear
Now to His altar draw near,
Join in profound adoration."*

Father closed the mass by giving us his last blessing. We lined up in the aisle, while he dipped the tips of his fingers in a golden dish of holy water. He made a cross on our foreheads, saying, "In nomine Patris et Filii et Spiritus Sancti," which means 'In the name of the Father, the Son and Holy Ghost'. Then he spread his good hand on our heads.

"Go in peace my child."

Albertus and his two altar boys made their way back to the sacristy, us girls made our way back to our dormitory and the visitors were left talking amongst themselves outside the church.

The Concert

Sr Ursula clapped her hands together.

"Girls, get changed. Zhose who are to help in zer kitchen, Banner, Glenysen Sprattsen, Sally, Lynn, Zelda, Poppy, Zhelma, hurry up oontz go to help Sister Gertrude getting zer food out to zer dining room, because everyone vill eat before ve have zer concert.

"Zer visitors are already making zheir way to zer dining room. You ozzer girls are to line up outside zer dining room alongside zer boys, until I komm to open zer doors up oontz let you in. Now hurry up girls, quick quick! I vant to go oontz let our visitors in."

With that she left us scurrying around getting changed.

"Hey Banner what did you dig me in the ribs for, in church? That hurt," I sang out while I was pulling my tunic off. Banner giggled.

"I didn't mean to, Sprattie." Then her face changed to anger. "That was the farmer who told on us when we ran away, unna, Thelma and you girls? That was his farm we went to, hey?"

All the other girls who'd run away with Banner agreed.

"Here Sprattie, do my buttons up." Thelma came over to me, turning her back so I could button her dress. "Gee Banner, I hope they don't send me to work on his farm. You seen the horrible look he had on his face when we glanced back at him in church. If Father does send me there I'll kill all his chooks and steal his food." We all had a good laugh going to the door, for once leaving the dormitory like a bomb had hit it.

Walking into the kitchen we were told, "Hurry up oontz start taking zer pots of food to zer serving table Glenysen oontz Nancy oontz May. Put zhese white aprons on oontz start serving zer visitors as zhey are all seated. All zer ozzer children are already in zer dining room, Zhelma you are to serve zer brothers, who are sitting amongst zer boys. Fazher Albertus vill be brought into his special chair by zer altar boys."

So we got busy serving the food. First up were big crockery bowls of soup with ladles on the table so the visitors could help themselves. There was activity going on all around us, the nuns were busy serving the other kids, when Sr Ursula rang the hand bell and everyone stopped.

Jimmy and Teddy walked with Fr Albertus, each holding onto one of his elbows. We all started clapping and cheering as they led him to his favourite wooden armchair, which the brothers had brought over from the monastery as a surprise for him. It was the one he used to sit in while listening to the evening news. Now it was pushed up to a table among the boys. Father stood at the chair, his face breaking into a smile. Then he fumbled in his trouser pocket and his left hand trembled as he pulled out a wrinkled hanky to wipe his glasses, holding them up and squinting to see if they were clean.

"Zhank you for my favourite chair, you children. It iss a very nice zhought of you." He bowed his white head, explaining that there was a lot of dust around which made his eyes water. "Now ve vill say Grace before we eat, zhen ve vill haf the concert, and after zer concert all you children vill get a revard."

We were feeling very happy because we had heard what we wanted to hear. Every time Father had a special occasion like a birthday he'd give us chocolate. After Grace it didn't take visitors and children long to finish eating and it was about seven o'clock when we cleared away the tea dishes.

The boys spruced up the dining room and drew the long tables to one side. All the benches were out for us kids to sit on, with chairs for the visitors, sisters, priests and brothers down the front. We had a special place for Father's armchair, right in the middle of the aisle which divided girls from boys. In that way we were all around him.

When everyone was settled, the girls from earlier times went behind the stage to get ready to open up the concert with our song. It was the one we sang to any visitors who came to the mission, and to the nuns, brothers and priests when they arrived from Germany. First we helped Br Edward to light twenty kerosene lanterns and secure them around various points of the stage.

Sr Ursula went in front of the curtain to give her speech of welcome, explaining what the concert was for. "So sit back everyone oontz enjoy yourself, oontz zhere vill be after zer concert a cup of tea. For Fazher oontz zer visitors." With that she clicked her heels, clapped her hands and went to switch the main lights off at the wall.

Br Edward drew apart the thin white sheets which served for curtains and the setting of the bush scene with painted kookaburras looked real in the glow of all the lanterns. Sr Erika, at the back of the stage where she couldn't be seen, gave us the chorus on the old piano.

Every now and again we'd put our heads down and rub the floor with our slippers in front and, ducking down quick-way behind our mates' backs, lift the bottom hem of our dresses to wipe our sniffles. Sr Helga stood in front on her tiptoes, conducting us with her mouth open wide and a wooden ruler held up in front.

> "Kookaburra sits in the old gum tree-ee,
> merry merry king of the bush is he-ee,
> Laugh, Kookaburra, laugh ...
> Kookaburra's life is gay and free!"

Everybody got up and clapped and cheered when we finished. Us girls took off shame-way before the curtain was drawn. We stood in the dark at the back of the stage and waited for the boys to do their play. Teddy and Jimmy held a grey army blanket up lengthwise. Gerry and Jason hid down behind it and Mallee came out to recite in a singsong voice, "I hope you like our play, we'll do our best in every way, to please and make you laugh."

Mallee was a scrawny boy and we did laugh at him, making fun of his bony frame and big black eyes. Gerry and Jason had a pair of old boots on their hands and they waved them over the top of the blanket. We actually did think they were clever doing handstands. All the other boys were singing, *"Ta-ra-ra boom te ay!"*

After the boys, ten girls were to sing individually. I had my turn with *No Fairer Land*. Somehow that used to upset me, especially the words of the first verse,

> *"No fairer land lies far and wide*
> *than this our own dear countryside."*

Banner was last. She shocked us all. Instead of the song she was supposed to perform, she said she had a poem. Everyone went deadly quiet, watching Banner with her head down only glancing up now and again and rubbing her foot on the floor.

> *"I wish to say goodbye to you, Father.*
> *Thanks for all the marbles*
> *and lollies that you gave us.*
> *I didn't mean to get into trouble all the time,*
> *and I know you didn't mean*
> *to hit me all the time.*
> *Me and the other girls are going to miss you*
> *and the lollies and marbles."*

With that, Banner stood there quiet, smiling. Everybody clapped and laughed. She ran off the stage and came to join the rest of us in the dark. When we went out for our final song, Thelma whispered to Banner and me to look at Fr Albertus, "The dust must be getting in his eyes again."

Mother Superior spoke from the stage, "Zer girls oontz boys oontz sisters all vish you vell for zer future. Many zhanks for everyzhing. Ve oontz zer children vill alvays pray for you and you vill never be forgotten."

Then she announced the final song, *The Happy Wanderer*. Everyone joined in as we sang,

> *"... along the mountain track,*
> *and as I go, I laugh and sing,*
> *my knapsack on my back,*
> *val d'ree, val d'rah, val d'ree,*
> *val d'ra-hahahahah ..."*

Back in the dormitory we sat on Banner's bed, munching our chocolates.

"Choo Banner, you were brave to say that poem to Father, unna you girls?" I looked around for support. They were all busy eating.

Thelma piped up, "Was you frightened?"

"Course I was frightened. I don't know what came over me, but it was good afterwards, even though I felt shame and took off from the stage."

Read Your Story

We were a group, situated right at the back of the classroom in a corner, which suited me because we were close to a window. Half the time my concentration was out the window with the birds and butterflies in the garden. I hated doing sums. One of my worst subjects, it used to drain everything out of me. Half the time I sat there and scribbled, making out I knew what I was doing, especially when I saw my mates burst out crying, holding their heads and putting their faces down onto the desk in pain. Mr Pitts had a habit of throwing dusters from wherever he was standing in the room. That turned me right off sums.

I was petrified of asking how to do anything. It meant standing up in front of the whole class and being laughed at by everyone. As we could not do the work, our little group cheated off one another. When Mr Pitts marked the papers he found we all had the same mistakes. Rather than pimp on one another, we would all end up with a thrashing, and a promise that if it ever happened again, we could all expect worse.

As the months went on my interest in most school subjects just wasn't. The other kids felt the same, we remained in a dull, gloomy state. We went with the flow, when we were in school with Mr Pitts.

Another two boys joined our group, Benji and Patty. They came from the wheatbelt area and were brothers. Their scrawny type fitted in quite nicely, they were like Jimmy and Billy, very spirited and full of mischief. We seemed to suit one another perfectly.

It got to the stage, every time Mr Pitts gave us a lesson about different subjects and would ask one of the kids from our group to stand up and answer a question, we would become the centre of attention. Everyone would laugh and think it was a great joke.

It never worried the rest of the class whether we were included in some subjects or not. The only ones who took it up for us and felt something for us were Sally and Poppy.

My favourite subjects were reading and writing. This particular day, we were all given the next edition of the *School Paper,* which was a monthly magazine, with stories continuing every month, about the early explorers.

Mr Pitts explained that we had to write, for a topic, on a certain explorer from the *School Paper.* He had done wonders out in the desert, finding waterholes and making discoveries along the rabbit-proof fence, with certain people, Aborigines, who were his helpers.

What got me was this other story, over the page, about the Australian Aborigines, how they lived in the desert, in what they called maya-mayas, bark shelters. When it came time for putting pen to paper, I was so excited that I wrote all about the Aboriginal people, how they went out searching for berries.

I wrote it in line with what we used to do in our spare time, thinking it was me out picking berries, because we used to love going for gumnuts and mistletoe fruit and looking around for things in the bush. We collected the hard brown gumnuts from the ground and knocked them until their black seeds fell out, or picked the seed out with a piece of wire.

The mistletoe bunches were always right up on top of the trees, so we would use our gings or big sticks to knock them down. The mistletoe was small, with a yellow skin when it was ripe. We peeled this or squeezed them until the white stringy part popped out. It was very sweet.

There was also a tree with thick crusty bark and as we walked we could see the pale gum shining on it in big round lumps. We collected them in rusty jam tins. If they were too hard we knocked them off with rocks. Inside, the lumps were soft. We took the gum back in tins to the kitchen and while the nuns were at prayers, we found an old pot, sneaked into the storeroom and robbed a handful of sugar. Then we mixed the gum with sugar and water and boiled it up on the stove to make toffee.

Some girls couldn't wait for it to cool down and burnt their mouths. All the time we were nervous that the nuns might catch us.

"Quick, baalay, Sister comin' quick." Girls used to give false alarms as someone was running out with a handful of sugar and she wouldn't know what to do with it, whether to go to the pot and drop it in or run back to the store with it. So she would spill it over the floor.

"Sorry sister girl, Sister not comin' I'm only makin' out." And she would end up getting punched for that. If any sugar spilled on the stove it would burn black and the nuns would know. They could tell from our mouths if we'd been eating it, because the gum left a whitish stain around our lips.

I also included in my story that if it was not for that black man showing that white man certain things out in the desert, he might have got real sick, or lost, or died. I couldn't understand at the time why they walked around naked, because the nuns told us that it was very bad and sinful to show your body bare to anyone, and that was a mortal sin.

During the morning session Mr Pitts interrupted our writing with a break for Piece time, our morning tea. Mr Pitts explained that after Piece time, we were to read out our stories.

The bell rang and we all filed back into the class. When everyone was seated he called this girl Annie out, to read her story. Annie was his pet, as far as we were concerned. She was real clever and sometimes I used to envy her, for she always seemed to get everything right. As usual when she finished reading Mr Pitts told us all to give her a clap for saying the right thing and what an excellent story she had written. She strutted to her seat like a proud peacock.

"Glenyse Spratt, come to the front and read your story."

As usual, everyone burst out laughing.

"Be quiet!"

I took no notice, got to the front of the class and glanced up at my mates. They were all smiling, so in a loud voice I began to read the story about my people, how they used to be happy taking food back to the camp, to feed their kids. Mr Pitts banged his stick on the table. I jumped and nearly wet myself.

"What a lot of rot, Glenyse Spratt!"

The whole class burst out laughing.

"Don't you ever take any notice of what I am trying to teach you? We are talking about the white explorers who gave great service to this country of ours, not those people you are writing about. I tell you what, Glenyse Spratt, you ought to thank your lucky stars that you are not out in the scrub eating berries or whatever they eat! You should be thankful you are in a nice home with good decent people to look after you."

He grabbed the story out of my hands, ripped the paper into little bits and let them flutter down to the floor.

"Now bend down and pick up this rubbish, place it in the bin and get back to your seat! I'll help you along."

I felt his boot as I bent down to gather up the torn pieces of my work, and went to my seat feeling shame, the laughter of the kids all around me. Florry grabbed and squeezed my hand under the desk.

"Sprattie, you right. Why don't you cry?" she whispered.

"At least I made them all laugh."

Everyone Roared

During one of our morning sessions with teacher in his usual mood, we were interrupted and told to put our nib pens down, sit up straight in our desks and fold our arms. Not wondering too much about what was in store for us, because we were used to Mr Pitts' sudden doings, I put my pen down and sat up like the rest.

Then for some reason or other I couldn't help but feel a little uneasy. My knees started knocking and Florry dug me in the ribs, to stop my knee bumping hers. Mr Pitts bellowed.

"I am going to call out ten names and as soon as I call your name I want you to come out the front and stand in line."

And the first name called out was mine. I jumped up and rushed to the front. My uneasiness started to disappear. I was thinking he must have something good in store for us, for it was not usual for me to be the first one called out. I thought his ideas about me must be changing, I must be doing good work after all. What did seem strange, he didn't seem angry any more but continued on with a faint smile about him.

"Florry, Billy, Sally, Poppy."

When I saw all my mates getting called out I started to feel really pleased and stood up proudly in my position, first in line out the front. Our gang usually copped it every day and it wasn't like us to be called out together. When there were ten of us standing in a row, Mr Pitts walked slowly down the front of us, holding the long cane waddy at his back. He reached the top of the line where I stood, swivelled round on his heels and gave us all that smile.

"Well, I suppose you must be wondering what's going on, and why I called you out. Well I'll tell you why. Since I have been teaching here for a year and a half, nearly two years now, because this year is coming to an end and that will make it two years for me, I have found it very hard to get through to this group that is standing here in front of me."

As he looked back at the rest of the class I noticed some of the others smiling, so I gave them one of my cheesy grins, not realising the irony of Mr Pitts' speech. He looked back at us, and kept pacing up and down with the waddy still held at his back.

"I feel as if I have wasted my time with you lot," he suddenly poked Billy in the stomach. "Billy Rice, what would you like to do when you leave school?"

Taken aback, Billy stuttered and muttered about how he would like to become a shearer and work on a farm with his dad. Everyone roared laughing. Mr Pitts went on down the line, asking everybody what they would like to do when they left school. The other kids in the class thought it was a good joke, laughing at our gang's future plans. Mr Pitts poked me in the ribs.

"And what would you like to do, Glenyse Spratt?"

The schoolroom was silent. I glanced up quickly and they were all waiting, with eager smirks on their faces. I felt like a clown in a circus. Again Mr Pitts poked me in the ribs and my whole body shook. I hummed and harred, shame-way, my head down.

"I dunn—no."

"Oh, you don't know, hey?" He poked me again. "Let me see," Mr Pitts went on in a happy smiling mood, "you could become a doctor or a schoolteacher like me." By this time the whole class was in uproar, as I kept jumping every time I got a poke from his cane.

"Well, what is it, Glenyse Spratt? You seem to be the one who thinks you have all the knowledge, what do you think you're best at? What do you like doing?"

"I like reading and writing."

"Now before you go any further, one thing I must tell you is you can't read, your spelling is up the creek and as for writing, you'll never do it, you can't even write your name properly.

"Let me tell you something, all you lot standing in front of me. There is no future for you, you can forget all about that which you have just told me and the rest of the class. There is no hope for you, you are going to end up back in the camps where you came from! You are wasting my time. Now go back and sit down."

The rest rushed back to their seats but I just stood still. I knew full well that I was going to cop it, but deep down inside me something kept bugging me about what Mr Pitts had said: that we would all end up back in the camps we had come from. Everybody else was sitting back in their seats.

"What is the matter with you?" Mr Pitts came roaring at me. "Do you want me to give you a hand back to your seat?" He grabbed me by the scruff of my dress. I quickly crouched down and put my hands over my head, so I wouldn't cop it there. The kids were laughing again as Mr Pitts started shaking me.

"I only want to know what a camp is. I've never been to a camp."

"Get back to your seat." He shoved me stumbling down the aisle. I lost my balance and fell beside the desk, dress over my head. Florry leaned over and flicked it down. I crawled up on my seat not knowing which way to look till I saw my sister Sally smiling at me.

Through the Door

One night we were sitting on a bed when Rina came over.
"Is Mr Pitts all right to you girls?"
"What do you mean, Rina?" Poppy asked.
"We told you, he's too strict," Zelda protested.
"I don't mean it that way," Rina spoke quietly. She was a working girl and it wasn't like her to come and ask questions. She was very reserved in her ways.
"You know, you fullas – " Her face was going shame and she started tying a knot in the bottom hem of her pyjama jacket.
"Choo Rina," Florry said, "what you going shame-way for? What you trying to tell us, hey?"
Rina suddenly lifted her head, looked at us and flung her hands up. "You fullas can't be all that silly. Haven't you noticed Mr Pitts' ways towards Rebecca?"
We all said, "Who Rebecca?"
Now Rina was getting impatient with us, "You know her, won't nothing sink in your heads? She the girl that left Mr Pitts' class early in the year, that because me and her will be same age soon, sixteen, we both became working girls together."
"Oh you talking about our mate Silkie." We had nicknamed her that because her face was smooth like a baby's. We became so used to calling one another by our nicknames it seemed strange to use our straight names.
"Yeah, what about her?" We were all getting curious now.
"Well, you fullas, watch Rebecca when she serves the teachers their evening meal. Take good notice of the smile on her face as she walks through the dining room, and also take notice when you fullas finish school in the afternoon."
Rebecca was the cleaner of our schoolrooms, that was one of her jobs.
"Watch them when no-one else is around, I'll take you there and show you what I mean. Don't you see, you slow learners?

They are boyfriend-girlfriend. They are in love!"

"How do you know?" we all asked.

"I saw them kissing in the classroom the other day, when I walked past Father's dining room." Her words knocked the stuffing out of us. I remembered how Silkie had twirled herself around and hugged me in the dormitory, on the day we all saw Mr Pitts for the first time in church.

"Hey Rina, don't tell us fullas any more, choo, I don't want to get in trouble for talking rude about anyone."

I really liked Silkie, she was kind to me. Of course Banner started laughing and making fun as usual.

"Hey, Rina, I'll come with you tomorrow after school and have a peep at them, who else is coming?" I immediately sat back and never said a word, quietly listening to the rest of them making plans how they would sneak through the big dining room when the nuns went down to the convent for afternoon tea. All the kids would be out playing in the fields. School finished at three.

The next day, after school, sweet innocent me found myself with the rest of the gang. There was no brother or priest in sight, they were either at the dairy or in the monastery, which were both some distance away. The girls walked past the dining room to where the back door of the school was situated. In the dark alleyway, pressing on the door, we were trying not to make too much noise but everyone was quietly pushing and shoving.

As usual, Banner took over the whole show and was really bunging it on, giving us the details. Crouched over the keyhole she described the whole intimate scene, making us all pull at one another to get a look. After getting us all excited, she would give us a brief look and then shove us out of the way. Suddenly she whispered.

"Ohhh waa ..."

"What, Banner?"

"Hey choo ... choo, he's kissing her."

We all surged forward on the door, which could not take our weight any more and burst open. Rebecca jumped off Mr Pitts' lap as he stood up. We found ourselves in an embarrassing position on the floor on top of one another. I was almost too shame to look at his red face.

"Whose idea was this?" he quietly asked. We all started putting the blame on one another.

"Right, you other girls from my class, if you know what's good for you, you had better disappear! Rina Ball and Banner Spalding, you are two working girls, you stay behind."

The rest of us bolted out to the fields and sat under a redgum tree, sweating it out, fearing the worst from the nuns when they found out. Poppy and Florry and I wished that Rina had never told us. Banner and Rina came from the classroom, reached us and squatted down, rubbing their hands. We could see that Rina had been crying. Her eyes were red and there were marks all over her arms from the cane.

It was a real shock for Rina to be hit by sir because she was a working girl and had nothing to do with the teachers.

"Don't cry, where was Rebecca when he flogged you?"

"He sent her outside. She went back in as we was coming out." Banner took it as a joke, even though she too had been hit.

Through the following weeks I could not look Mr Pitts in the eye, and I noticed that sometimes, when he spoke to us, his eyes were darting everywhere but on us. He could not look straight at us any more. I was so glad that there was only one month left until Christmas. I wanted to leave. Deep down in my heart I knew that I was no good for school any more.

It didn't come as a surprise when our gang was lined up

outside the fathers' dining room along with the rest of the class. Father Ludwig announced that he would pick who was going to Perth to a boarding school, to further their studies, and who wasn't going. The ones he picked were praised, with a certificate and warm handshake, from both Father and Mr Pitts. The ones not picked each received the cane across both hands. The girls were told their lives would be only good for washing pots, and the boys for the dairy. So we saw the year out.

How Long Were You Girls Here?

In the mid-1960s I was a working girl, helping Sr Gertrude in the kitchen. All girls, school and working, were in the bathroom changing one morning, when we were told that a new priest was arriving. By this time many of the earlier priests and brothers had gone, except for Br Roland, Br Joseph and Br Edward, who still looked after the dairy. Sr Ursula continued on with her usual run-down to us about a new arrival.

"Girls, ve have a new priest arriving zhis morning, who iss going to be zer new rector, like Fazher Albertus vas. If you are out in zer school playground, you are not to crowd around zer car, if it happens to turn up. You girls are to stay avay. Mother Superior vill make our new priest velcome. During zer veek you vill all meet him, and I am sure zhat you vill all understand him, vhen he talks to you. You von't have any trobble understanding him."

"Why, Sister?" Any newcomer to our mission brought an anxious time for us kids, we were all so curious to find out what sort of person he or she would turn out to be. After we fell all over them, then the novelty would wear off when we found they were just as strict as the rest of them and we would keep our distance.

"You see girls," Sr Ursula went on explaining, "zhis priest ve have coming here, he iss not from our home in Shermany. He iss from Australia. Therefore you vill be able to understand him, not like vhen ve nuns first arrived from Shermany, you may remember. A few of zer older girls, Glenysen Sprattsen oontz Florry Jacks, you may recall our first days vhen ve spoke, vasn't it, girls?"

"Yes Sister," we giggled as all the other girls stared at us. I was thinking how silly this must look, her trying to explain how they had sounded trying to pronounce words to us, and the irony of it all. Suddenly the bell rang.

"You may go now girls, oontz remember vhat I said! If you disobey my orders you vill be punished."

As all the other girls ran to take positions in line to enter their classrooms, Florry and I walked slowly back over to the kitchen talking. It would be different hearing a voice other than a German one for a priest.

"You never know, Sprattie, he might not be so strict like this mob."

"I hope not." I opened the kitchen door. Sr Gertrude blasted us straight away.

"Komm girls, hurry up viz your shobs. You know ve have a new priest arriving. It iss getting late, he might be here around morning tea time. Glenysen Sprattsen hurry up viz zer cake mix so zhat ve have zer cakes ready. Florry Jacks, you come over here oontz make bread and dripping for zer children's Piece time."

Florry and I got stuck into our jobs and thought nothing of the matter. I made up the chocolate mixture, put it into the long cake tins and carried these to the big oven of the wood stove. Florry was spreading the dripping. I leaned up near Florry, gave a quick glance around to see where Sr Gertrude was, grabbed a piece of bread, wiped it around the dripping bowl and stuffed it in my mouth.

"Sprattie, stop that, you know what will happen if Sister catch you."

"Choo Florry, I couldn't help it, I'm starving girl." I turned towards the window and wiped the crumbs from my face, so Sister wouldn't cotton to anything. "Baalay, Florry, choo quick, Br Edward just turned up from Perth with that new fulla." Florry came and leaned on my shoulder.

"Where, Sprattie? Get out of my way, I can't see."

"There look." Brother climbed out of the driver's side and from the other came a tall man.

"Look at him, what he's wearing, Sprattie. His clothes! Choo, he look half undress." We had only seen priests and brothers in long pants and their black habits. This man was in shorts.

I was still at the window watching, when the school door opened for Piece time and the kids tore out madly to line up under the gumtree for their bread and dripping. Sr Gertrude's voice erupted.

"Komm avay from zer window, ach girl, can't you smell zer cake? It iss burning!" With her finger and thumb clamped around my ear, she pulled me along to the oven.

"Now get zhis cake out and put it on zer cooling rack. Hurry, girl. Brother Edward iss already here viz zer new priest and you stand around here gazing! Vhat's viz you, girl?" She left me with my ear burning more than the cakes had, as I bent over the open oven.

Sr Gertrude scuttled off muttering to the cupboard where the big stainless steel teapots were kept. When I finally had everything ready I carried the cake up to the fathers' dining room and set the table with white plain cups and saucers and serviettes. Back in the kitchen Florry passed me a mug of milky tea.

"How is your ear?"

"Still ringing." I could see that she wanted to laugh.

"Sorry but I can't help it, when Sister was dragging you by the ears, you should have seen your face." Then we both cracked up laughing.

"Come on Florry, finish your tea, then me and you jump up on the sink, let's have a look out the window at the new priest. That mob are still outside playing!"

So we hopped up on the sink and looked out at the kids milling around in the yard and the sisters talking to the tall man in shorts. All of a sudden we saw Sr Gertrude pointing in our direction.

"Baalay, they coming our way," Florry said.

"They just coming for morning tea," I told her. We both jumped down and ran to our jobs. We were flat out working when they walked in, on their way up to the dining room. As Sister strolled in with the new priest, we stood real close beside one another, making out we were washing up, listening to Sister explain all about the kitchen to him.

"Zhis iss vhere ve cook all zer food, oontz zhis iss zer storeroom vhere ve keep everyzhing. Oontz zhis iss our two vorking girls, Glenysen Sprattsen and Florry Jacks. Girls, meet zer new Fazher." Father came over smiling and held his hands out to us.

"Hello girls, I am Father Bob Maxwell." Straight away, our heads went down and our feet started rubbing the floor. "How long were you girls here?" We couldn't speak. Sr Gertrude spoke for us.

"Zhese are two of our earlier girls. Zhey came to us as tiny little ones. Now zhey are vorking girls."

"Oh, I see," Father said. "I'll catch up later with you, girls." And the procession made its way up to the dining room. Soon as they left, Florry and I lifted our heads up.

"He seemed different, unna Sprattie?"

"What about when he held his hands out to us? I felt shame, that's why I turned away." In later life, I met Fr Maxwell and learned that he couldn't believe it when he came to the mission that day. He thought he had walked into another world. A world of the past.

Changes

In the following months Fr Maxwell took over the running of our home. Our clothing changed from long khaki dresses to modern skirts and tops, shirts, shorts and slacks.

After wearing ankle-length dresses and big baggy bloomers since we were knee high to a grasshopper, it was all so strange and daring to us to be walking around in shorts and short skirts. We were handed our pairs of dark blue shorts and light blue pullover blouses in the bathroom by Sr Ursula.

The look on her face when handing them out was very strained. "Girls, you are to put zhese shorts on for all your sports, and vhen you have finished doing your sports, already I have spoken viz zer teacher, zhat you are to come back to zer bathroom oontz have your shower oontz put on your school uniform oontz hang your shorts up again. Oontz you older girls vill put on your vorking clothes, zhen go to your shobs in zer kitchen."

We felt shame because they seemed shorter in the legs than our bloomers.

"Choo!" We giggled and mucked around, making fun of one another's legs. Having put my shorts and blouse on, I sat down shame-way on the bench in the corner and waited for the rest of the girls to get ready.

"Sprattie, you got solid legs," Paula sang out.

"Gurn, shut up you fullas, look at your own sticks. Hey Tilly, wait till Teddy see those knees, he'll be proper mardong for you."

Tilly hardly ever spoke. When anyone talked to her, she'd put her head down and walk the other way. Therefore she was often a target for us girls. Soon as I sang out, Tilly ran in amongst the other girls and crouched down.

"Hey, hey Tilly, don't get shame, we only teasing you."

"Girls! Line up at zer door oontz zhen go to your exercise

oontz I vill see you back here for your showers after," Sister shouted, still with that strange look on her face.

Mr Pitts was waiting with the boys when we reached the fields. Straight away, when they saw us, the boys started sniggering behind Mr Pitts' back and pointing to our legs. We were fuming inside but had to turn a blind eye, as we followed down to the boys' field. Us girls walked in a group, all bunched up so tight we were tripping over one another. Mr Pitts turned around.

"You girls, stop being so stupid, and walk in front of me. Who do you think you are? You are all nobodies. There is nothing special about you lot, that you have to run and hide all the time. That's just being typical of the race of people you come from."

I did not understand what he meant, I just kept walking with the rest of the girls in front of Mr Pitts' beady eyes. And so we reached the boys' playing fields. All our growing years this was out of bounds to us girls but my uneasiness soon changed when I saw the looks of discontent on the boys' faces. We did our work-out on their swings and bars!

We soon forgot about our legs and really rubbed it into the boys, as their equipment was better than ours for a start, and we felt the nuns, brothers and priests favoured them by giving them better swings than ours. We didn't mind the heavy work-out, we just had pleasure seeing the looks on their faces as we swung higher and higher on their bars, knowing that they couldn't say anything.

At other times girls sneaked into their paddock and played on their swings when no-one was around. If they caught the girls at it, they would get them on the ground and punch into them, but the girls could handle themselves and give just as much punishment as the boys dealt out.

Quite often, when visitors arrived, we would sneak around the dining room window to have a look at them and how much they had on the table. When the visitors went the girls had to clean up after and we would have silent fights for the leftover biscuits and cake. Normally we would get biscuits and cake on rare occasions like one of the nun's or brother's feast days.

Banner made a habit of lifting a small girl up to the window while the rest waited around squatting on the ground. The small girl had to watch the people eating and report how much of the cake and biscuits was left, telling us everything.

"Five biscuits left now, no more cake now."

If there were leftovers we'd get really happy, but if the small girl sang out, "The last biscuit gone," Banner would drop her flat and she'd walk away sore and disappointed with the rest of us.

One day there were some visitors and we were told that it was Rebecca's birthday. Although we weren't invited, as usual we couldn't resist looking in the dining room window.

Rebecca was all dressed in white, and there was Mr Pitts standing beside her. Fr Maxwell and Fr Ludwig were there and some old man and woman, whom we later found out to be the parents of Mr Pitts. It did not dawn on us what was really taking place. Later one of the older girls put us in the picture about the wedding. That same year Mr Pitts left with Rebecca.

Fr Maxwell made a lot of changes. No more school at the mission, and two brand new buses arrived. They took the remaining children to neighbouring schools in the district. For all our picnics we were now driven around in the buses, by Father or one of the working boys. No more Our Lady's old truck.

And the following year, Rina and Banner left the mission to work for white families on their properties. Like all the other goings away there was no party. Florry and I remained that year, to see most of the nuns gone. Sr Gertrude continued in the kitchen, and Sr Ursula looked after us.

When Banner left we all missed her very much, we cried for her a long time. Her spirited character had played a big part in our lives. After the loneliness we carried on regardless. Sally my sister and Poppy went with her. They were our family. Only Florry and myself were left of our gang from earlier times. All the boys of our gang were gone too.

Jinny Come Lately

Beatles music was belting out all over the world. I was a big girl now, a teenager. Although we still had that strict mission style in us, I was taking more interest in the pop music. I felt they had more rhythm and excitement than boring old hymns, although the hymns had meaningful messages.

The nuns used to preach to us in a way where I think they wanted us to grow up to be nuns like them, for want of a better way of life, in the Christian way of upbringing.

I remember how at night time, when lights were out, Sister used to go down to the convent and we would sneak around the old wireless on which Sister used to listen to the news. We'd sit quietly tapping away to our favourite Beatles numbers and songs from other pop stars and Country and Western singers. Chains, Del Shannon, Bobby Bare, Miller's Cave, were my favourites, along with Johnny Tillotson, *Send Me the Pillow that You Dream On*. But there was one which I used to go mad over – Bryan Hyland, *Jinny Come Lately*.

We weren't allowed to sing those songs. The nuns said they were forbidden because most of them were about lust and sex. Although we didn't know much about that in those days, I remember some of the girls went real mad over their pop stars, some of the bigger girls.

They came back from holidays with books all about the lives of pop stars. Those were forbidden too but the girls sneaked them in. That didn't worry us! Everything I was given about Bryan Hyland I treasured. I used to carry his picture around with me anywhere I went. I tucked it in my bra and at night sitting around the wireless, the other girls would dig me in the ribs when his song came on, saying how solid I was. I used to think I was just it, holding it up in front of myself and crooning over his picture. I went to sleep with Bryan Hyland under my pillow.

One day Florry, myself and a couple of other working girls had the job of peeling buckets and buckets of potatoes. Sr Gertrude sent us to set ourselves up under the old gumtree, not far from the kitchen, as there was a bench around this bit of a rockery which we kids had made. We usually peeled potatoes in the kitchen around a big steel tub, splashing plenty of water on the floor when we chucked the peeled potatoes into the tub. Sister said that the floorboards were rotting.

We didn't mind, we felt free out there, at least we could talk. We were humming Beatles songs when Florry said, "Sprattie, what's that song you like? How does it go now? Can you hum it for us?"

"Course I can, how could I forget my favourite?" I chucked my potato into the bucket, stood up and brushed all the peelings off my dress. Then I reached into my bra and took out my photo of Bryan Hyland. The girls were all looking at me.

"Hurry up, Sprattie, before Sister come."

"Give me a look at the picture," Florry said, so I passed it to her steady-way.

"You can all have a look while I sing. Just tell me if you see Sister coming." I remained standing with my back towards the kitchen in order to face them. I thought it was important for me to stand, seeing I was singing my favourite song. Everybody went quiet, I coughed a bit to clear my throat and started to sing.

"*I only met you just a couple of days ago ...*"

"Oh solid," said Florry, and she handed my picture back to me as I was still singing:

"*... sweet sweet as can be.*

You only have to smile, and in a little while —"

A rough hand reached from the back of me and snatched my picture. I went real cold. Sr Gertrude's voice bellowed in my ear.

"Vhat iss going on, Glenysen Sprattsen? Ach girl, vhere did you get zhis evil picture from?" She ripped it to pieces in front of me and I felt my ego crumble. I started to tremble, my knees went weak.

"How dare you sing zhis dirty rude song!" All the guilty feelings rippled through my body and I felt my face going hot and cold. I covered it with my hands so I couldn't see the other girls, although I felt their looks go right through me.

"Girl, you are to come viz me to see Mother Superior. You ozzers get a move on oontz finish peeling zer potatoes. Zhen carry zer pot back to zer kitchen. I vill see you all zhere!"

She stormed off with me, clutching the back of my dress, pulling and pushing me along with her. Head down, I went to the dormitory, where I was left to wait for Mother Superior. She was soon preaching to me about how evil and sinful it was, and about my body, how we should keep it pure and how sinful people sing about their personal parts. I was finally told to be first one at confession, to tell Father, and to beg forgiveness from God so that I could wipe all filthy thoughts out of my mind, to make me pure again.

My mates crowded around me on my bed that night, all pressing for news. What happened to me? and what did Sister say? I refused to talk for a while, still choked up.

"Why didn't you let me know she was coming? Especially you, Florry, you supposed to be my best mate."

"Sorry my sister, we was all looking at you thinking that you was solid, we was just gunna sing with you, when it was too late."

"Never mind, what I don't like is having to make confession and say what I have been singing to you mob."

"Choo Sprattie, what you mean?"

"I got to tell that new young priest what I sang. That's gunna be real shame." After Mother Superior's lecture and the way I felt, I didn't think I could talk to a man.

The following Saturday afternoon I found myself at confession, reciting in a shaky voice my song to Fr Maxwell. Just as well the curtain was between us and I couldn't see his face. After I had repeated the song, Father didn't speak for a while. I felt like running out of the confessional box. The quiet was nerve racking. When he did speak his words came out slow and gentle, which made me feel uneasy.

"Glenyse, could you repeat the second line of that song, please?"

*"I only met you
and I want your love and soul ..."*

That's what I thought it said then; the real last words were *"lovin' so"*.

"The person who sings this song is like a devil," Fr Maxwell responded. "He is an evil man possessing a young child's mind. There is no other person whom you can give your love and soul to other than to God. In a lustful way, this man is giving his soul to the devil. Do you really understand the Ninth Commandment?"

"Nah."

"You see, Glenyse, all these songs and words lead into this sin, the act of illicit sex."

I didn't have a clue as to what he was going on about, all I wanted to do was to bolt out the door and get away from him.

"Glenyse, I know how you feel. There comes a time in your life, when you will find you are not a little girl any more, your body is developing into a young woman and so your whole attitude changes, especially when you are around boys. Your feelings toward a boy become different, you begin to be attracted to him and he to you."

Then, out of the blue, he asked me, "Did a boy ever touch you? or kiss you?"

Not having the faintest idea about what he was going on

about, I said, "Nah, they not allowed to talk to us girls and us girls not allowed to talk to them. We play in our own fields."

"All right, I'll give you your penance. But on Monday I will arrange with the Sister in charge to start giving you girls talks on sex, especially now that you are working girls. We must not have you leaving the mission not knowing the real meaning of the Ninth Commandment: 'Thou Shalt Not Commit Adultery'."

So I left the confessional box in a state of confusion, wondering why Father didn't jar me up the way Sr Gertrude and Mother Superior had. I couldn't concentrate on saying penance because I didn't understand why Father should say all those terrible things about what I thought was a beautiful song. Why was I feeling so strange inside me? I should have been feeling really dirty but somehow or other, for once in my life, I felt on top of the world after this kind of lecture.

The Nativity

The carrying of the statue of Our Lady was a tradition in the very early years at the mission, when we were still very young. This continued to the late 60s. We'd start off the procession from the church, carrying Our Lady's statue around to every building in the mission. I marvelled at this statue, it was a yard in height, with white vestments and blue cloak. The expression on Mother Mary's face was so pious and serene and perfect, with her two hands folded together, that when I was a little girl I thought she was real.

Sometimes, when I had to help clean the church, I stood in front of the statue and moved from side to side. Her eyes seemed to follow me. I used to get scared. Although she was pretty, whenever I was near this statue, I would hide behind a friend and feel better that she was looking at my mate and not me.

We learned in our religious instruction that November was the time Our Lady was carrying for Jesus. So God had sent a star for the shepherds, which was like a message, to follow that star to Bethlehem. And we were told that the night of the 25th of December, the star stopped over a certain barn, and that was where Jesus was born in a manger.

So every week from the middle of November till Christmas Day, the nuns would pick out a special boy or girl to help carry the statue, the one who was best behaved for the week. That meant no swearing, being considerate of others, helping them with their duties without being asked and going to church in the mornings during the week without being asked. I never qualified in these categories, all my time at the mission. Not that it worried me, as long as God still loved his sinners. I still prayed at night and asked forgiveness.

Letti was a newcomer, she'd been with us six months. She was very tall and pretty, with long black hair. Letti walked around with her nose in the air and had her particular friends with the same attitude. She stood in front of the altar that evening and waited till the last hymn was sung. Then Father gave his sermon about the special time of the year having come again for carrying Our Lady's statue, and he chose Letti to carry it. This year the statue would go to the big girls' dormitory first, then the little girls' and so on until the final night, when it was to be carried to the dairy, to be placed in the Separating Room.

Father walked slowly down the aisle behind Letti, with two altar boys either side bearing lighted candles. Then we girls formed a line and the boys followed, then the sisters and brothers and priests in procession, singing hymns and praying as we all went along.

In the girls' dormitory a special place on top of the mantlepiece was decorated with wild bush flowers and fresh roses, white, dark red and yellow. When the statue was finally standing in its place, with sisters, brothers and priests standing around us in the dormitory, we said the Rosary and there was a re-enactment of what took place, concerning the shepherd and stars and Our Lady. Then after prayers everybody would file out, leaving us to prepare for bed, and the statue would be with us for a week.

The next week we'd go through the same routine of carrying the statue to the next building, until on the final night, Christmas night, it stood back in the Separating Room of the dairy, which was all decorated with gumtree leaves. The nuns made candle cups, putting coloured paper around them, blue, green and red. Each one of us held a candle in one of these cups, from the fathers down to the smallest. Bales of hay were set down on the cement floor, where we all sat, with the smell of the cow yards and the calves mooing.

The brothers brought in a couple of lambs and tied them in the corner with a bale of hay to munch on. We never had a donkey to tie up in the barn, the animal that Our Lady actually rode around on. Br Edward would bring in our pet cow and tie her up to a post in the corner. It was Golden Star. She was so gentle the girls used to ride on her when they were small.

Alongside Golden Star were our other two pets, Hum-bla, a sheep, whom we'd brought up as a baby and who used to follow us around wherever we went, and the dog called Uss-ter, which made me think of Poppy.

Uss-ter had been given to Brother by one of the farmers who regularly came to our church. Uss-ter's fur coat was jet black. His real name was Buster, but because Poppy had stuttered, she used to get stuck on the beginning of the word and could not pronounce it. When we threw a stick for Buster he would bring it back and Poppy used to jump up and down singing out, "Uss-ter, Uss-ter!" So we copied her. Uss-ter got used to his name, and the name stuck with us.

There we were, standing once again in the Separating Room, with all the trappings of a nativity scene. Some of the boys and girls were dressed up as shepherds and angels. The three brothers, Roland, Joseph and Edward, were the three wise men. Florry and I stood side by side at our usual spot, under the gumtree saplings that the brothers had cut and erected in the corner of the room. That year was lonely for us, because our closest mates were gone. Without them it was not the same.

Christmas always felt sad to me. It should have been a happy time, with our Christmas party and presents to come. In one way it brought everyone together, brothers, sisters, priests, boys and girls. Then in another way, most of the kids with whom we made good friends and got to love during the year were suddenly gone. Even if it was just for holidays, you did not know if you would ever see them again.

As we joined in with everybody singing *Silent Night*, I glanced around the room at the different girls and boys. My thoughts took me back to earlier days. Where these new kids were standing and singing, that's where Poppy, Sally, Thelma, Banner and all our mates had stood.

Then I started wondering, "Where are they? What are they doing?" And my eyes began to get blurry. The last verse of *Silent Night* was being sung.

> *"All is calm, all is quiet,*
> *round yon virgin mother and child,*
> *holy infant so tender and mild,*
> *sleep in heavenly peace,*
> *slee-eep in hea-venly peace ..."*

Florry and I held hands and joined in bravely. I was thinking that Poppy and Banner and the rest of the gang would have wanted us to be happy.

In the middle of the following year it was my turn to go out and work for white people. I left with the sisters' blessings. Florry and I both had a good cry when we said goodbye.

Later, a couple of letters came to my place of work from Florry, telling me that all the sisters and brothers had left and Fr Maxwell was getting new homes built so that kids who were coming later were being cared for by house parents, in a family style of living. No more dormitory style.

For years after leaving the mission all of our group had to face the outside world in a struggle of trying to cope. We faced abuse and torment at the jobs we came up with, because of our lack of knowledge, being brought up not knowing who we were, or where we were bound, or what lay ahead of us.

Glossary

Nyungar words used in this book:
Spelling of these words varies according to area. In this list, the spelling used by the author is followed by some alternative accepted usages for the more southern region.

The title phrase of the book, 'unna you fullas', means 'isn't that rignt, you fellows?'

baalay, baali	look out, warning
choo, tju	exclamation of disbelief, shame
goona, guna	excrement
jirruping, djurubiny	happy, keen on, likes, wants
koondang, kurndang	shy, ashamed
mardong	loves, attracted to
maya-maya	house, shelter
moorditj, murditj	solid, good, really good
mumaries	spirits
Nyungar	name for an Aboriginal language group of South West Australia
unna	isn't that right, do you think so too?
wadjala, wadjela	white person
winyarn, winyan	sorrowful, pitiful, sad sight
yorga, yorkka, yokka	woman

Nyungar language consultant: Glenyse Collard

Other special words:

bob	slang for a shilling
camp pie	tinned meat/cereal loaf
catseye	clear playing marble, with colour inset
Dettol	a disinfectant
Dingo brand	a flour trade name
fullas	fellows
ging/shanghai	hand-held catapault
oh waa	expression of alarm
peewee	small playing marble
possie	good position
ringie	a game of marbles played in a circle
shilling	earlier coin, worth ten cents
sookie	weak, complaining child
sus	test, inspect
tombowler	large playing marble
torn collar	white patterned playing marble
waa	what, where? Expression of alarm
waadow	what about that, what do you reckon?
waddy	broad stick for punishment
wirly	rippled glass playing marble